Pastor Chefs

40 Day Marriage Challenge

Creating Quality Time in Your Marriage by Creating Quality Food in Your Kitchen

Pastors Bill and Cynthia Malone

SIGNALMAN PUBLISHING

Pastor Chefs 40 Day Marriage Challenge
by Bill and Cynthia Malone

Signalman Publishing
www.signalmanpublishing.com
email: info@signalmanpublishing.com
Kissimmee, Florida
1-888-907-4423

ISBN: 978-1-940145-34-1 (paperback)
978-1-940145-35-8 (ebook)

Library of Congress Control Number: 2014957251

Printed in the United States of America

Dedication

We dedicate this book to our parents, Rallan & Eva Malone, and Willie & the late Syddie Lawrence who taught us the value and importance of marriage. We would like to thank them for loving us even when we were not lovable.

We also dedicate this book to our children, Ryan Malone and Seneca Diggs. We've always believed in sowing seeds into our next generation and we pray that our marriage has been an inspiration to you and will carry on for generations to come.

We dedicate this book to God's perfect will and purpose in our marriage and for all that He has done with us and through us. Our prayer is that every couple who reads this book will find a nugget (no, not a chicken nugget) of spiritual truth that can be used to strengthen their relationship.

Pastor Chefs mission and vision is not about the food (although it is AMAZING) but rather it is about the relationships and the increased commitment to developing quality time in marriage. For everyone who has prayed for us and who continues to believe in the vision that God has placed in us, this book is for you... God is not done yet. Hang on, this is going to be a lot of fun!

Contents

INTRODUCTION

Love begins at home, and sometimes it begins in the kitchen. At the top of every year our church joins together in a time of fasting and prayer. Now please understand, that our fast is not a total fast, it's more of a partial fast where we modify our diets and commit our lives and time to this effort. The Daniel fast is a good example of a partial fast. As a pastor I've always enjoyed these types of fast because it forces people to "talk" about what's acceptable to eat during the fasting period and what's not acceptable to eat during the fasting period. Thus creating opportunities to fellowship and have discussion as to how God is moving in their lives and bodies during their own personal time of fasting.

My wife and I are always looking for new ways to motivate and encourage people to support ministry, especially when we're convinced it will benefit them spiritually and emotionally. This year we decided to create a series of YouTube videos of us cooking fast safe meals. We named these videos "40 Days of Fast Safe Meals" (not super creative, but it worked for us). Our hope was that people would enjoy watching their pastors cook so much that they would see that serving God could be fun and would at some point begin fasting themselves. Unfortunately, this did not go over as well as we had hoped or expected. In fact, most of the people (including the ministers in our church) pretended they didn't even see the videos and acted as though we had a third eye in the middle of our forehead when we would even mention this effort. It was a little discouraging to say the least, but we fought through that and continued to cook together, every single day for 40 days.

To be honest, I think we both wanted to quit on about day 10 but, both of us were thoroughly convinced that God gave us the idea and thus it became a mandate from God that we saw it through. This took a great deal of personal commitment from both me and my wife, because there were a few days in this effort where we had absolutely lost the will to continue. There were days where we would get in from work late, or just find that we were personally exhausted for some reason or another. There were several days where we were bickering with one another over some household issue that left neither of us in the mood to cook together and then video the process and put it on YouTube. There were a few nights that we found ourselves cooking at 2 or 3 in the morning, so that we could meet this obligation to upload a cooking video that no one was going to watch the next day. As I'm sure you could guess, this only made it that much harder to press our way to completing these 40 days of cooking. It was a very long 40 days.

A funny thing happened on the way to 40 days of fast safe meals. I discovered that I actually enjoyed cooking meals with my wife, and she might not admit it, but I'm pretty sure she enjoyed it as well. I don't want to say I enjoy cooking in general, but I did discover that I honestly and deeply enjoyed being in the kitchen with the first lady in my life. Over this period of time, In addition to discovering a new love for food that I cooked myself, I felt the beginning of new bonds and connections with my wife. These were connections that somehow had been missing, that quite honestly; I didn't even notice were missing, until the sparks of this new relationship began to ignite flames that had somehow lost its heat.

When the 40 days of pressure and cooking was over, I actually found myself missing the time with my wife. I missed the food and the conversation. I missed the challenge and connection

This new connection opened my eyes to the importance of creating dedicated **Priority Time** with your spouse.

For the purpose of this book, let's define **Priority Time** as time spent with your spouse that overrides all other issues and concerns. That means, regardless of how you feel or what's on your schedule, your **Priority Time** assignment *must* be completed before you close your eyes for the night.

Although this book is for married couples, I believe the concepts we're going to discuss would be helpful for any couple hoping to ignite (or reignite) a spark in their relationship. I know a lot of couples that are going through the ringer right now, some who think they've tried everything, some who are convinced that nothing short of a miracle can save their marriage or relationship. Some who are now on that unfortunate treadmill of pretending to be happy when their hearts are broken. It is my contention that if you give 40 days of dedicated effort into your relationship, you will see returns come back to you in ways you never expected. Sometimes you just have to trust God.

This book is a challenge to every married couple that feels the need and the desire to connect or reconnect with one another. This is a challenge to set aside your own personal time and your personal activities for **Priority Time** with your spouse.

40 Day Marriage Challenge

If you complete the challenges for all 40 days, you will notice a closer connection with your spouse, you will be better able to handle the stressors associated with being in a relationship by learning to press through them, and you will enjoy AMAZING dishes that you cook together.

If you and your spouse accept this challenge, here's what you will need to do:

- Be willing to put off making any major relationship decisions (as in should I stay or leave) for at least 4 to 6 months. Once the 40 days are complete, allow your new attitude and new routines to set in and change your marriage.

- Start taking an honest look at yourself and your relationship.

- Make each day with your spouse and the completion of each challenge your most important priority for the day. (*Priority Time*).

- Prayerfully work through each challenge. If you are able, record yourselves cooking and watch it later.

- Yes, it is important that BOTH spouses participate. This challenge is designed to bring you closer to your spouse by using BOTH of your desires to reconnect and re-energize your relationship.

- **Don't quit!** You *will* want to quit because there will be times that it is just not convenient to complete a day's challenge. **DO IT ANYWAY.** If your marriage is the priority, then press through without regard to convenience.

40 DAY MARRIAGE CHALLENGE:

- **PRIORITIZE** daily prayer and devotion with your spouse.
- **PRAY** together, touching and agreeing for God to move in your family.
- **READ** prescribed scriptures to one another (not alone or apart).
- **COOK** together following the recipes *to the letter.*
- At the end of each day **REFLECT** on the challenge and how you **FEEL** about what you did that day.

Just in case you forgot:

Priority Time: Time spent with your spouse that OVERRIDES all other issues and concerns. Again, that means, regardless of how you feel or what's on your schedule, your **Priority Time** assignment *must* be completed before you close your eyes for the night.

40 Day Covenant Agreement

Please Sign and Agree

Our Commitment:
I commit to completing this 40 day challenge with prayer and with honesty. I will do my best to complete all 40 daily assignments. I commit to being faithful and honest with my spouse throughout this process. I commit to giving my relationship **Priority Time** *within each challenge activity. I will make certain that this process remains at the top of my priority list and schedule, and when the process is difficult, I will press on.*
For Forty (40) days we agree to **pray together, read together, and cook together** *and at the end of each day we will make a personal marriage declaration over our family.*
I understand this pledge is a reflection of my commitment to this relationship.

_____ *Date* _____

_____ *Date* _____

What do you think will be the hardest part of this challenge?

What do you think will be the hardest part of this challenge for your spouse?

Pray together:
Lord, thank you for giving me the courage to accept this challenge for my marriage. I am thanking You in advance for giving me the strength to see this through to the very end. I have made up my mind today, that my marriage is important enough for me to give it priority over my job, my friends, my hobbies, or any other worldly concerns. In Jesus' name I surrender my own efforts and my own goals to You and commit to giving **Priority Time** *to You Lord and to my Marriage. I accept this challenge in Jesus' name. Amen.*

CHALLENGE ACCEPTED

CHALLENGE DAY ONE

He and all his family were devout and God-fearing; he gave generously to those in need and prayed to God regularly.
Acts 10:2

The Bible doesn't tell us exactly *when* or *where* or *how* Cornelius prayed. It doesn't tell us whether he prayed in the morning, during the day or at night. It doesn't tell us whether he was on his knees or on his feet. But what it does is tell us that he prayed regularly and that his whole family was devout before the Lord. The Bible tells us that his family was God-fearing and was generous to those in need. You never know when God is going to INVADE your life and disrupt your regular routine, but you can live in holy expectation and anticipation, knowing that God is orchestrating a supernatural harmony in your home.

DAILY PRAYER

Before you get out of the bed, before you brush your teeth, before you do anything that is a normal part of your morning routine. Turn to your spouse, don't sit up, don't get up, simply turn over and pray. Ask God to be a part of your morning. Ask God to give you the strength to make early Morning Prayer a normal part of your life and relationship.

DEVOTION

Our relationship to God should foster marital closeness, and nothing brings us closer to God or each other more than prayer. Praying together is the most powerful weapon a couple has to true connection. Why is it so rare that couples regularly pray together?

Husband READ to Wife: Romans 15:5-6

Now may the God of patience and comfort grant you to be like-minded toward one another, according to Christ Jesus, that you may with one mind and one mouth glorify the God and Father of our Lord Jesus Christ.

Challenge Day One Declaration

We declare and decree God's incredible blessings and mercy over our marriage. We expect to see an increase in personal connection, love and joy in this relationship. We expect to experience love at a level that God intended for us to have from the beginning. We trust God that today will be the first step in a stronger more satisfying relationship.

Wife READ to Husband: John 17:20-23

I do not pray for these alone, but also for those who will believe in Me through their word; that they all may be one, as You, Father, are in Me, and I in You; that they also may be one in Us, that the world may believe that You sent Me. And the glory which You gave Me I have given them, that they may be one just as We are one: I in them, and You in Me; that they may be made perfect in one, and that the world may know that You have sent Me, and have loved them as You have loved Me.

MARRIAGE CHALLENGE

Think about your schedule and your daily activities. Are you willing to do whatever it takes to spend quality and priority time with your spouse? Write down your plan, and be specific.

Pastor Chefs Maple-Glazed Salmon

CHALLENGE DAY 1
PASTOR CHEFS
RECIPE
(COOK TOGETHER)

Remember to follow this recipe to the letter. It's not about the meal; it's about the *priority time* that you spend together.

Ingredients:
2 salmon steaks cut in half with skin on
2 tbsp of intimacy (real tenderness, be as intimate with one another as possible during the cooking of this meal… have a little fun with this)
1/4 cup pure maple syrup
2 tbsp soy sauce
3 tbsp fresh ginger minced
1 tbsp of politeness and a pinch of kindness
   (you're going to need this for all 40 days so have an ample supply available)
1-2 green onions diced fine
1 tbsp butter

Directions:
In a container large enough to fit the fish in one layer, mix syrup, soy sauce and ginger. Add fish and coat well. Marinate fish for at least four hours and up to a day in the refrigerator flipping every so often. Heat oven to 365 degrees. Rub your spouses back and shoulders.

In a large oven-safe frying pan heat butter and sear salmon on the tops. Flip salmon so the skin is down and cook for about two minutes. Pray and then Pour any remaining sauce over the tops and cook in oven until done to your liking. Kiss your spouse and then stir in tenderness (to taste), Remove pan from oven, cover and let fish rest for 10 minutes, it will continue to cook a bit so do not overcook it in the oven. Garnish with green onions and kindness and serve.

Before you sit down to enjoy your tender salmon, give your spouse the most gentle and emotionally tender kiss you can generate.

Day One Challenge Reflection

The Pastor Chef Challenge is 40 days of praying together, reading together, and cooking together. Close the day with a *Family Declaration!* Reflect on your prayers and praise God for the day.

Praise Report:

_____

_____

_____

_____

How does today's scripture apply to your family?

_____

_____

_____

_____

How was the meal? Did you make any changes (write it down)

_____

_____

_____

_____

What is God saying to you?

_____

_____

_____

CHALLENGE DAY TWO

By faith Abraham obeyed when he was called to go out to the place which he would receive as an inheritance. And he went out, not knowing where he was going.
Hebrew 11:8

If you're waiting for the perfect moment to set things right in your marriage, prepare to wait for a lifetime. The perfect time will never come. The perfect moment for a good conversation, the perfect moment for that intimate time alone to set things straight will never come. You'll never be financially, emotionally, or spiritually in a perfect position to make things right. There will always be a good excuse to put off fixing your relationship. At some point all you can do is trust God and go where He tells you to go and do what God tells you to do. God is not waiting for you to be ready; He's ready for you to just go.

DAILY PRAYER

Before you start your day, before you leave your room in the morning, hold hands and PRAY:

Lord, I pray that You would strengthen my spouse to resist any temptation that comes their way. Remove temptation especially in the area of (ask your spouse what they need help with). Make my spouse strong today in every area that they are weak. Help them to overcome and tear down ANY stronghold that exists that may have a negative impact on our relationship. AMEN.

DEVOTION

There is only ONE path to unity, oneness, and a successful marriage and that is the path that leads to a mutual dependency on Jesus Christ and the confidence that God has the lead in your marriage.

Husband READ to Wife: Psalms 55:22

Cast your burden on the Lord, And He shall sustain you; He shall never permit the righteous to be moved.

Challenge Day Two Declaration

We declare and decree that we WILL experience God's love and faithfulness in our marriage. We will trust God and not doubt His power over our relationship. We will trust in Him, knowing He cannot and will not fail us. We will allow our marriage and our testimony to be an encouragement to others. We will surrender our lives, heart, and relationship to be used by God. Our marriage WILL be an instrument for God to use to reach others.

Wife READ to Husband: Proverbs 3:5-6

Trust in the Lord with all your heart, And lean not on your own understanding; In all your ways acknowledge Him, And He shall direct your paths.

MARRIAGE CHALLENGE

Do you feel like your spouse is all there for you emotionally? If so, tell your spouse how much you appreciate them, if not, explain and find ways to fix this very serious issue.

Pastor Chefs Glazed Honey-Bourbon Salmon

Remember to follow this recipe to the letter. It's not about the meal; it's about the *priority time* that you spend together.

Ingredients:
2 6oz Salmon fillets
1 tbsp melted butter
1 cup of self control (you will need it with this dish)
1 tbsp honey
1 tbsp emotional support (you'll have to explain why you need this)
1 tbsp bourbon (to taste)
3 tbsp pepper jelly (apricot jalapeno recommended)

Directions:
Preheat oven to 350 degrees F.
Mix together bourbon liquor, honey, melted butter, and pepper jelly until evenly incorporated.
Place salmon fillets in a glass dish and coat with mixture.

Hug and kiss your spouse and then place the salmon in the oven and bake 30-40 minutes, or until easily flaked with a fork. Pray and then top with self control (you're going to need it).

Before you sit down to enjoy your meal, turn on the music and dance.

Day Two Challenge Reflection

The Pastor Chef Challenge is 40 days of praying together, reading together, and cooking together. Close the day with a _Family Declaration!_ Reflect on your prayers and praise God for the day.

Praise Report:

_____

_____

_____

_____

How does today's scripture apply to your family?

_____

_____

_____

_____

How was the meal? Did you make any changes (write it down)

_____

_____

_____

What is God saying to you?

_____

_____

CHALLENGE DAY THREE

A man's heart plans his way, But the Lord directs his steps.
Proverbs 16:9

Sometimes it may feel as though your relationship has come to a standstill and has stopped moving forward, but it has not. God has a clear and active plan for your marriage. There comes a point where you have to make up your mind that you're going to trust the all-mighty, all-knowing, all-powerful God with your marriage. You're going to have to accept that the all-mighty, all-knowing, all-powerful God knows what He's doing. You're going to have to accept that the all-mighty, all-knowing, all-powerful God has a plan for you and your relationship. Trust Him to get to the big steps and the small ones too. He will keep you moving forward, if you let Him.

DAILY PRAYER

Before you start your day, before you leave your room in the morning, hold hands and PRAY:

Lord, I pray for you to open the doors of physical affection between my spouse and me. Allow us to open our hearts to one another and lay aside our past issues that have blocked our freedom to live openly and affectionately towards one another. Lord, change our habits of indifference and apathy so that we can begin to walk in and live in the marriage you called us to enjoy since You personally, with your mighty hand, brought us both together. AMEN.

DEVOTION

Who was the first to say I love you today? Try to beat your spouse to the "Love Punch." Begin each day with words of affection and love. Try compliments and words of affirmations, love on your spouse with your words and your heart. Because a lack of love and attention will kill everything else you try. It just will.

Husband READ to Wife: Song of Solomon 1:15

*The Beloved Behold, you are fair, my love! Behold, you are fair!
You have dove's eyes.*

Wife READ to Husband: Song of Solomon 1:16

The Shulamite Behold, you are handsome, my beloved! Yes, pleasant!
Also our bed is green.

MARRIAGE CHALLENGE

When you and your spouse are emotionally challenged or faced with a major conflict, do you get emotional or do you tend to withdraw? How do you and your spouse deal with conflict together?

Pastor Chefs Jerk Salmon

Ingredients:
3 Salmon steaks (about ½ lb. ea.)
1 lb. of goodness and courtesy
   (you might need more than a pound, use your own judgment)
2 tbsp jerk marinade*
1 tsp salt
1 tsp. dried pepper flakes
½ tsp thyme leaves
1 tbsp lemon juice
1 tbsp sugar
1 tbsp kisses… (Now go give your spouse a little sugar)

Directions:
Wash salmon and arrange side by side in an oven proof baking container. Combine 1lb. goodness, marinade, salt, pepper, and thyme. Rub seasonings over fish. Sprinkle or squeeze lime juice over fish. Sprinkle over sugar. Broil in center of oven for 20 minutes.

**Before you start eating your meal, go put on your pajamas…
have fun with this** ☺

Remember to follow this recipe to the letter. It's not about the meal; it's about the *priority time* that you spend together.

Day Three Challenge Reflection

The Pastor Chef Challenge is 40 days of praying together, reading together, and cooking together. Close the day with a *Family Declaration!* Reflect on your prayers and praise God for the day.

Praise Report:

_____

_____

_____

_____

How does today's scripture apply to your family?

_____

_____

_____

_____

How was the meal? Did you make any changes (write it down)

_____

_____

_____

_____

What is God saying to you?

_____

_____

CHALLENGE DAY FOUR

And Joshua said to the people, "Sanctify yourselves, for tomorrow the Lord will do wonders among you.
Joshua 3:5

There are too many people right now looking for God to do wonders in their lives without first being willing to sanctify themselves. For a marriage to be blessed it must first be sanctified. Consecration means you're giving up control and letting God call the shots. We should learn to give God final authority over every family decision. His Word is the final word. His Word is the final say in every situation. His Word is the compass we use to guide us through the storms in life that inevitably complicate our marriages and relationships. Consecration is saying NO to your own flawed personal plans and YES to God's divine ambition for your relationship.

DAILY PRAYER

Before you start your day, before you leave your room in the morning, hold hands and PRAY:
Lord, I pray that You will not allow us to entertain confusion in our minds. But that You will give us both, spiritual clarity. Please, Lord, keep us from being tormented with impure, evil, negative, or sinful thoughts. Enable us to be transformed by the renewing of our minds. Lord, let us focus on whatever things are true, noble, just, pure, lovely, of good report, having virtue, or anything praiseworthy, let our minds stay on those things in our marriage. AMEN.

DEVOTION

Society does not honor or appreciate the godly values of fidelity, trust, selflessness, temperance, and loving devotion. A successful marriage is one that is built on the rock solid foundation of God's loving values and connections.

Husband READ to Wife: Proverbs 5:21-23

For the ways of man are before the eyes of the Lord, And He ponders all his paths. His own iniquities entrap the wicked man, And he is caught in the cords of his sin. He shall die for lack of instruction, And in the greatness of his folly he shall go astray.

Challenge Day Four Declaration

We declare and decree that it is not too late to have a satisfying marriage. It is not too late for us to accomplish all the things God has placed in our hearts and spirits to accomplish. God has a plan for our relationship and has opened His windows of favor and blessings. He is about to release a special anointing over us to help us accomplish our family dreams. This is our time! This is our moment! This is our day.

{ 26 }

Wife READ to Husband: Hebrews 13:4

Marriage is honorable among all, and the bed undefiled; but fornicators and adulterers God will judge.

MARRIAGE CHALLENGE

24 hours NO SCREENS:

No TV, No computers, no tablets, No cell phones. Give this time to your spouse.

Pastor Chefs Homemade White Chocolate

Ingredients:
4 cups of milk of your choice
   (or you can substitute heavy cream or half and half, or do a mixture)
1 tsp. vanilla extract
8 oz. white chocolate, chopped into small pieces (or white chocolate chips)
whipped cream or marshmallows for topping
A whole lot of comfort

Directions:
Stir together milk, vanilla and chopped white chocolate in a medium saucepan. Cook over medium-low heat, stirring occasionally, until the white hot chocolate comes to a simmer. (Do not let it come to a boil.) Remove from heat and serve immediately, topped with whipped cream, lots of comfort or marshmallows if desired.

While enjoying your hot chocolate together, dim the lights and passionately look into each other's eyes. (Don't stop passionately looking into each other's eyes until all of the hot chocolate is gone)

Remember to follow this recipe to the letter. It's not about the meal; it's about the *priority time* that you spend together.

Day Four Challenge Reflection

The Pastor Chef Challenge is 40 days of praying together, reading together, and cooking together. Close the day with a *Family Declaration!* Reflect on your prayers and praise God for the day.

Praise Report:

_____

_____

_____

_____

How does today's scripture apply to your family?

_____

_____

_____

_____

How was the meal? Did you make any changes (write it down)

_____

_____

_____

_____

What is God saying to you?

_____

_____

CHALLENGE DAY FIVE

Every place that the sole of your foot will tread upon I have given you,
as I said to Moses.
Joshua 1:3

Pray until something happens. Pray until your situation changes. Pray until you see God moving all around you. Pray until you're out of breath and energy and need to go to sleep. Pray until God opens a door. Pray until your victory is clear and your testimony changes someone else's life. This is the level of determination you should have every single time you start praying for your family and for your legacy. Make up your mind that you will NEVER stop praying until God gets the glory from your prayers and faith. Trust Him, especially when you're praying for your family.

DAILY PRAYER

Before you start your day, before you leave your room in the morning, hold hands and PRAY:

Lord, I pray that You will unite me and my spouse in a bond of friendship, commitment, generosity, and love. Remove from us any immaturity, hostility or feelings of being inadequate for my spouse or relationship. Help us, Lord, to love each other enough to make time for one another. Help us Lord, to nurture, prioritize, and renew in us the emotional and loving connections that brought us together in the first place. Lord, let our love grow so great and so strong that it becomes a part of the legacy we leave our children. AMEN.

DEVOTION

Stable marriages produce healthier people. God knew exactly what He was doing when He created the institution of marriage. It is just not good for man (or woman) to be alone. Marriage allows two people to grow emotionally and spiritually into one loving, anointed, caring and spiritually connected person that can share and reveal to the world the love and joy that can only come from knowing a loving and living God.

Challenge Day Five Declaration

We declare and decree a legacy of love, peace, and faith over our entire family. We declare that we will store up blessings and anointing for our children. Our lives will be marked by excellence and integrity, because we will be committed to setting strong examples for our children to follow. The windows of heaven's blessings will be open unto our family and for all of the future generations to come, because we are so blessed.

Husband READ to Wife: 1 Corinthians 12:1-6

Now concerning spiritual gifts, brethren, I do not want you to be ignorant: You know that you were Gentiles, carried away to these dumb idols, however you were led. Therefore I make known to you that no one speaking by the Spirit of God calls Jesus accursed, and no one can say that Jesus is Lord except by the Holy Spirit. There are diversities of gifts, but the same Spirit. There are differences of ministries, but the same Lord. And there are diversities of activities, but it is the same God who works all in all.

Wife READ to Husband: 1 Corinthians 12:7-11

But the manifestation of the Spirit is given to each one for the profit of all: for to one is given the word of wisdom through the Spirit, to another the word of knowledge through the same Spirit, to another faith by the same Spirit, to another gifts of healings by the same Spirit, to another the working of miracles, to another prophecy, to another discerning of spirits, to another different kinds of tongues, to another the interpretation of tongues. But one and the same Spirit works all these things, distributing to each one individually as He wills.

Pastor Chefs Monkey Bread

OK, let's be real, there are very few things better than waking up to the smell of baked cinnamon in the morning.

Ingredients:
4 small (7.5 ounce) tubes of refrigerated buttermilk biscuits.
   (Cut each circle of dough into ¼'s)
2/3 cup sugar
2 tsp cinnamon
1 cup light brown sugar
1 stick of butter or margarine
½ dance around the room….first her then him
   (yes, it will look silly, but it's going to be fun, go for it)
Prepare a greased bundt pan

Directions:
Preheat oven to 350°F.

Place 2/3 cup sugar and 1 tsp. cinnamon into a ziplock bag. Add dough quarters, few at a time, to bag and shake until well coated. Place coated dough into Bundt pan. Continue this step until all dough is used.

In a small saucepan, add butter, brown sugar, and remaining 1 tsp. of cinnamon. Heat to melt butter and stir to combine well. Bring to a low boil. Stir constantly for 1 minute while boiling. Remove from heat, and pour over dough in Bundt pan.

Bake in oven for 25-30 minutes. This is a great place to add the dance, this is going to be so much better if you both are able to laugh while you cook. Let cool for 10 minutes and flip out of pan onto serving dish. Serve warm and add 2 kisses on the cheek of your spouse

Before you start enjoying your sweet snack, critique each other's dancing.

Remember to follow this recipe to the letter. It's not about the meal; it's about the *priority time* that you spend together.

Day Five Challenge Reflection

The Pastor Chef Challenge is 40 days of praying together, reading together, and cooking together. Close the day with a *Family Declaration!*
Reflect on your prayers and praise God for the day.

Praise Report:

_____

_____

_____

_____

How does today's scripture apply to your family?

_____

_____

_____

_____

How was the meal? Did you make any changes (write it down)

_____

_____

_____

_____

What is God saying to you?

_____

_____

CHALLENGE DAY SIX

The wind blows where it wishes, and you hear the sound of it, but cannot tell where it comes from and where it goes. So is everyone who is born of the Spirit.
John 3:8

God has a surprise for your marriage up his Holy sleeves. Whatever you're going through you just have to learn to trust that God knows what He's doing and let Him handle it. Miracles are nothing more than supernatural surprises that can only come from a God who has tricks that our small imaginations and perspectives cannot begin to fathom. The more you pray, the more you open yourself up to supernatural opportunities that come from God's holy surprises. Ask God right now to surprise you! He will.

DAILY PRAYER

Before you start your day, before you leave your room in the morning, hold hands and PRAY:

Lord, You are our refuge and strength, You are a very present help in the times of our marital issues. You have invited us to come boldly, hand in hand, to the throne of grace, that we may obtain mercy and the grace and love to help us in our time of need. Give us endurance to run this race and not give up on one another knowing that You will keep us in perfect peace with one another if only we trust in You. AMEN.

DEVOTION

If you have unmet needs, if you have unmet desires and concerns, if you have any issue that you feel you are lacking, don't underestimate the power of prayer. God is able to do things we could not even begin to imagine. Trusting God should be our default not our last resort. If you want to really see God move in your marriage and relationship, especially in the areas where you feel you are lacking, Trust God enough to ask Him for help. Prayer really does work.

Husband READ to Wife: Mark 11:24

Therefore I say to you, whatever things you ask when you pray, believe that you receive them, and you will have them.

Challenge Day Six Declaration

We declare and decree that God has a great plan and great purpose for our marriage. We declare that it is God that is directing our steps. We accept that there will be times that we won't understand why things are happening in our marriage, but we rejoice knowing that God is fully aware of not only knowing WHAT is going on in our situation, but also knows HOW we are going to come through it. We trust God and His perfect timing. We declare that trusting God will lead to blessings and peace in our relationship.

{ 34 }

Wife READ to Husband: James 5:15

And the prayer of faith will save the sick, and the Lord will raise him up. And if he has committed sins, he will be forgiven.

MARRIAGE CHALLENGE

Write a prayer for your spouse to read. Pray in agreement (find at least ONE thing to agree on in prayer) there is Real Power in agreement.

Pastor Chefs Early Morning French Toast

**CHALLENGE DAY 6
PASTOR CHEFS
RECIPE**
(COOK TOGETHER)

Ingredients:
1 tsp ground cinnamon
1/4 tsp ground nutmeg
2 tbsp sugar
2 Full and emotional kisses (give your spouse a little sugar)
4 tbsp butter
4 eggs
1/4 cup milk
1/2 tsp vanilla extract
8 slices white bread
1/2 cup maple syrup, warmed
1 large hug

Remember to follow this recipe to the letter. It's not about the meal; it's about the *priority time* that you spend together.

Directions:
In a small bowl, combine, cinnamon, nutmeg, and sugar and set aside briefly.

In a 10-inch or 12-inch skillet, melt butter over medium heat. Kiss. Whisk together cinnamon mixture, kiss, eggs, kiss, milk, and vanilla and pour into a shallow container such as a pie plate. Dip bread in egg mixture, kiss. Fry slices until golden brown, then flip to cook the other side. Serve with syrup. (this looks like another good place for a kiss)

Before enjoying this nice breakfast (lunch, dinner), give your spouse an early morning kiss

Day Six Challenge Reflection

The Pastor Chef Challenge is 40 days of praying together, reading together, and cooking together. Close the day with a *Family Declaration!* Reflect on your prayers and praise God for the day.

Praise Report:

_____

_____

_____

_____

How does today's scripture apply to your family?

_____

_____

_____

_____

How was the meal? Did you make any changes (write it down)

_____

_____

_____

_____

What is God saying to you?

_____

_____

CHALLENGE DAY SEVEN

...Write the vision And make it plain on tablets, That he may run who reads it.
Habbakkuk 2:2

Having a clear vision for your family is a powerful tool that will take your family far. Having a clear vision for your family that has been written down and shared with your spouse will take you to a whole new level of blessing and anointing. God commanded His prophet to write the vision down in a way that was plain and simple for everyone to see and understand. It's hard to run with something you can't see, take a moment with your spouse and develop a clear plan and vision together. Trust God, He will guide you and your family to the greater levels He has set aside for you and your family.

DAILY PRAYER

Before you start your day, before you leave your room in the morning, hold hands and PRAY:

*Lord, give me the vision for my family. I put our destiny in You, Lord, and our destiny into Your mighty hands. Show us if what we are doing now is what You want us to be doing or should we shift course to follow Your Will. Lord, we are in agreement that we want what You want for our family. We trust that **all things work together** for the good if we commit to loving You and are accepting of our purpose. Lord, we trust You with our future and surrender to Your lead and direction. AMEN.*

DEVOTION

Being in a marriage that God has blessed has a stabilizing effect on a person's behavior. A part of being married is planning for and looking forward to the future. Bringing children into the world and creating a legacy for them to follow. Married couples are more likely to be involved in their communities and tend to work harder to build and live in a stable environment. Your neighborhood, your community, and your world will be blessed because of your marriage.

Challenge Day Seven Declaration

We declare and decree that unexpected blessings are coming our way. We will move from a position of lack into a position of financial and emotional abundance. God will open doors and spiritual avenues for our family. He will give us favor with people that will bless us in unexpected ways. God will bless our family exceedingly and abundantly and beyond our expectations. **We are blessed!**

Husband READ to Wife: Proverbs 3:5-6

Trust in the Lord with all your heart, And lean not on your own understanding; In all your ways acknowledge Him, And He shall direct your paths.

Wife READ to Husband: Mark 10:6-10

But from the beginning of the creation, God 'made them male and female.' 'For this reason a man shall leave his father and mother and be joined to his wife, and the two shall become one flesh'; so then they are no longer two, but one flesh. Therefore what God has joined together, let not man separate." In the house His disciples also asked Him again about the same matter.

MARRIAGE CHALLENGE

"Write the vision And make it plain.." Spend some time with your spouse and *write* the vision for your family.

Pastor Chefs Chicken, Sausage and Peppers

CHALLENGE DAY 7
PASTOR CHEFS
RECIPE
(COOK TOGETHER)

Remember to follow this recipe to the letter. It's not about the meal; it's about the *priority time* that you spend together.

Ingredients:

2 tbsp unsalted butter

3/4 lbs sweet or hot Italian sausage, cut into chunks

3/4 lbs skinless, boneless chicken breasts, cut into chunks

Kosher salt and freshly ground pepper

1 tbsp whole wheat flour

1 small onion, chopped

1 prayer of agreement

2 Italian green frying peppers, cut into 1-inch pieces

3 cloves garlic, roughly chopped

1 Full measure of sensitivity

1/2 cup dry white wine

3/4 cup chicken broth

1 full measure of Faith

1/4 cup roughly chopped fresh parsley

2 jarred pickled cherry peppers, chopped, plus 2 tbsp liquid from the jar

Directions:

Heat 1 tbsp butter in a large skillet over medium-high heat. Cook the sausage until golden, about 2 minutes. Hug your spouse, express just how much you love them. Season the chicken with salt and pepper, then toss with the flour in a bowl; add to the skillet and cook until browned but not cooked through, about 3 minutes.

Add the onion, peppers, garlic, 1/2 tsp salt, and pepper to taste and cook 3 minutes. Add the wine, scraping up any browned bits; bring to a boil and cook until slightly reduced, about 1 minute. Add the broth and bring to a gentle simmer. Pray over your spouse. Cover and cook until the sausage and chicken are cooked through, about 5 minutes.

Transfer the chicken, sausage and vegetables to a platter with a slotted spoon. Increase the heat to high and stir the parsley and cherry peppers and their liquid into the skillet; boil until reduced by one-third, 2 to 3 minutes. Trust God for a better day. Hug your spouse and hold. Remove from the heat and stir in the remaining 1 tbsp butter. Pour the sauce over the chicken mixture.

Day Seven Challenge Reflection

The Pastor Chef Challenge is 40 days of praying together, reading together, and cooking together. Close the day with a *Family Declaration!* Reflect on your prayers and praise God for the day.

Praise Report:

_____

_____

_____

_____

How does today's scripture apply to your family?

_____

_____

_____

_____

How was the meal? Did you make any changes (write it down)

_____

_____

_____

_____

What is God saying to you?

_____

_____

CHALLENGE DAY EIGHT

Casting down arguments and every high thing that exalts itself against the knowledge of God, bringing every thought into captivity to the obedience of Christ.
2 Corinthians 10:5

Every couple has had at least one discussion that's produced a life changing idea, but it turns out that there are very few couples that leave these discussions with an action plan. The problem is that most couples follow up these life changing discussions about their amazing idea with an even longer discussion as to why they can't do it. They accept the arguments of failure before they ever even lift up their first prayer to an all powerful God. Trusting God implies that you pray and ask for His guidance BEFORE you accept defeat, even with those amazing ideas that pop into your collective minds. Trust God even with the secret plans that scare you.

DAILY PRAYER

Before you start your day, before you leave your room in the morning, hold hands and PRAY:

Lord, I trust You and look to You for everything that comes into my life. I trust you Lord with my dreams, my plans, my vision, my direction, my hopes, my fears, my children, my family, my spouse, my career, my education, even my thoughts. Thank you, Lord, for giving me the counsel I need to make good decisions. Lead me, Lord, to the right people and help me to avoid the ones that will give me bad counsel. I love you, Lord, and I thank You in advance for making me a wise person with good judgment. AMEN.

DEVOTION

Whenever we stop trusting God and give up on the spouses He gave us, we elevate a self-centered mind-set that esteems self-reliance, self-fulfillment and self-service above the unconditional love, joy, peace, forbearance, kindness, goodness, faithfulness, gentleness and self-control that can come from a healthy loving marital relationship.

Challenge Day Eight Declaration

We declare and decree that God will put our marriage on the fast track to blessings and will accelerate the plans He has created for our marriage. We will accomplish ALL of the dreams faster than we had expected or even thought possible. We declare that it will not take years and years to see God's blessings and revealed purpose for our relationship. God is moving in our lives faster and faster and faster. Victory is right in front of us, all we have to do is trust Him. **We trust Him!**

Husband READ to Wife: Ephesians 5:31-33

For this reason a man shall leave his father and mother and be joined to his wife, and the two shall become one flesh." This is a great mystery, but I speak concerning Christ and the church. Nevertheless let each one of you in particular so love his own wife as himself, and let the wife see that she respects her husband.

Wife READ to Husband: Proverbs 1:5

A wise man will hear and increase learning, And a man of understanding will attain wise counsel,

MARRIAGE CHALLENGE

On a scale of one to ten (with ten being the best), rate yourself on how well you listen to your spouse? (do you feel listened to?) Discuss.

Pastor Chefs Lemon Butter Chicken

Remember to follow this recipe to the letter. It's not about the meal; it's about the *priority time* that you spend together.

Ingredients:
4-6 skinless boneless chicken breast halves
1/2 cups of whole wheat flour
1/2 tsp sea salt
1 word of encouragement (feel free to give more if needed)
2 tsp lemon pepper seasoning
1/3 cup butter
2 sliced lemons
1 random act of humor (yes, we said humor. Have fun!)
2 tbsp lemon juice

Directions:
Using a meat mallet lightly pound each piece of chicken to 1/4 to 1/2 inch thickness (this is an important step don't skip it).

In a shallow bowl combine the flour and the salt... then coat the chicken breast with the flour mixture. Sprinkle chicken breast with lemon pepper seasoning. Tell a joke (this is another important step, don't skip it).

In a 12" skillet melt butter over medium-high heat. Cook chicken in the hot butter. 6 mins on both side until there is no pink remaining in the chicken (turn only once). Remove chicken from the skillet. Quick kiss. ADD lemon slices to the skillet; cook for 2-3 mins. or until the lemons are slightly brown (turn ONLY once).

Return chicken to the skillet, overlapping chicken breast slightly and arranging lemon slices around chicken. Drizzle with lemon juice. Quick kiss. Cook for 2-3 minutes or until the pan juices are reduced.

Transfer to platter (chicken and lemon slices) pour pan juices over the entire dish... (this dish is great with rice!)

Look your spouse in the eyes and share one thing you love about them, season with salt.

Day Eight Challenge Reflection

The Pastor Chef Challenge is 40 days of praying together, reading together, and cooking together. Close the day with a *Family Declaration!* Reflect on your prayers and praise God for the day.

Praise Report:

_____

_____

_____

_____

How does today's scripture apply to your family?

_____

_____

_____

_____

How was the meal? Did you make any changes (write it down)

_____

_____

_____

_____

What is God saying to you?

_____

_____

CHALLENGE DAY NINE

Continue earnestly in prayer, being vigilant in it with thanksgiving
Colossians 4:2

Without prayer it is very difficult to see God's movement in our lives. Too often we miss God's active hand over our lives because we're not actively acknowledging Him as a part of the things we do. Prayer is the difference between seeing with our natural eyes and seeing with our spiritual eyes. Prayer gives us a window into a God's eye view of our situation. When we start to see our life situations through God's eyes we start to see that our issues are not in our control at all.

DAILY PRAYER

Before you start your day, before you leave your room in the morning, hold hands and PRAY:
Lord, show us Your ways. Teach us Your paths. Lead us in Your truth and teach us, for You are the God of our salvation. There is nothing that is too difficult for You, Lord. Therefore we ask that You would enable everyone in our lives to come together for our personal good. Lord, I pray for divine intervention in EVERY situation that seems out of control. I trust You, Lord, and lay my life, my drama, my fears, and my doubts at your feet. AMEN.

DEVOTION

God does not want us to be more concerned with knowing the future then our concern with knowing Him. He wants us to trust Him to take our family into the direction that He has laid out for us. He wants us to trust Him wholly and completely. He wants us to surrender our will and our desires to Him. He wants us to know that He has our future in His hands. And He wants us to be OK with that.

Husband READ to Wife: Psalms 119:9-16

How can a young man cleanse his way? By taking heed according to Your word. With my whole heart I have sought You; Oh, let me not wander from Your commandments! Your word I have hidden in my heart, That I might not sin against You! Blessed are You, O Lord! Teach me Your statutes! With my lips I have declared All the judgments of Your mouth. I have rejoiced in the way of Your testi-

---

Challenge Day Nine Declaration

We declare and decree that God will do exceedingly, abundantly above all that we ask or think or even imagine. Because we honor God with our marriage, His blessings will pursue us and overtake us. We will see God in everything we do and every place we go. People will go out of their way to bless us because we are so covered with God's favor.

{ 46 }

monies, As much as in all riches. I will meditate on Your precepts, And contemplate Your ways. I will delight myself in Your statutes; I will not forget Your word.

Wife READ to Husband: Matthew 6: 25-34

Therefore I say to you, do not worry about your life, what you will eat or what you will drink; nor about your body, what you will put on. Is not life more than food and the body more than clothing? Look at the birds of the air, for they neither sow nor reap nor gather into barns; yet your heavenly Father feeds them. Are you not of more value than they? Which of you by worrying can add one cubit to his stature? So why do you worry about clothing? Consider the lilies of the field, how they grow: they neither toil nor spin; and yet I say to you that even Solomon in all his glory was not arrayed like one of these. Now if God so clothes the grass of the field, which today is, and tomorrow is thrown into the oven, will He not much more clothe you, O you of little faith? Therefore do not worry, saying, 'What shall we eat?' or 'What shall we drink?' or 'What shall we wear?' For after all these things the Gentiles seek. For your heavenly Father knows that you need all these things. But seek first the kingdom of God and His righteousness, and all these things shall be added to you. Therefore do not worry about tomorrow, for tomorrow will worry about its own things. Sufficient for the day has its own trouble.

Pastor Chefs First Lady's Smoked Salmon and Asparagus Wraps

CHALLENGE DAY 9
PASTOR CHEFS
RECIPE
(COOK TOGETHER)

Remember to follow this recipe to the letter. It's not about the meal; it's about the *priority time* that you spend together.

First, prepare the Mozzarella. (Whisk):
1/2 cup Italian salad dressing (any brand)
Add a little of God's blessings in this dish
1 tsp dijon mustard (any brand)
at least 8 slices of mozzarella cheese

Prepare the Asparagus. (Toss):
1 lbs of FRESH Asparagus, trimmed
2 tbsp olive oil (anoint your spouse with some oil while you're at it)
   (pastor likes to add salt and pepper at this point)

For the wraps:
4 whole wheat tortillas
sliced smoked salmon

Directions:
Preheat oven to 425.
Wisk together the Italian dressing and dijon, then pour over the mozzarella slices in a shallow dish. Turn mozzarella to coat with marinade. Pray. Set the mozzarella aside while preparing the asparagus.

Toss the asparagus spears with oil and season with salt and pepper, transfer to a baking sheet (roast asparagus until crisp and tender this will take about 10 mins).

While the asparagus is roasting in the oven, hug your spouse the entire 10 minutes (yes, the *entire* 10 minutes… Don't let go).

HEAT a non stick skillet (medium heat) Pray. Brush the inside of the tortilla with marinade, then top with 2-3 slices of marinated mozzarella, put on few slices of smoked salmon (to taste... pastor likes a lot), and a quarter of the asparagus. Tightly roll each wrap.

Brown wraps in the hot skillet until golden and the mozzarella slightly melts. Remove, slice in half, and eat (don't forget to pray over your food).

Day Nine Challenge Reflection

The Pastor Chef Challenge is 40 days of praying together, reading together, and cooking together. Close the day with a *Family Declaration!* Reflect on your prayers and praise God for the day.

Praise Report:

_____

_____

_____

_____

How does today's scripture apply to your family?

_____

_____

_____

_____

How was the meal? Did you make any changes (write it down)

_____

_____

_____

_____

What is God saying to you?

_____

_____

CHALLENGE DAY TEN

... Oh, that all the Lord's people were prophets and that the Lord would put His Spirit upon them!
Numbers 11:29

Have you asked God where He wants your family to go, have you asked Him to lead, guide, and direct the steps your family is to take? Have you asked God for a prophetic voice for your family? God did not create prayer for one way communication; He created prayer so that He could communicate His will to you and your marriage as well. When you open the lines of communication with God, you open opportunities for a prophetic voice to become an active part of your marriage and life. Speak God's voice over your marriage.

DAILY PRAYER

Before you start your day, before you leave your room in the morning, hold hands and PRAY:

Lord, we pray that You reveal to us what You want us to do and enable us to do it well. Lord, we don't want our own dreams and plans for the future to get in the way of what You want for us. We know You desire mercy and gaining a knowledge of You more than You want our petty sacrifices. We long to know You more and to conform to the image of your Son in our marriage. Thank you, Lord, for creating us for a purpose, thank You, Lord, for allowing us to worship You. AMEN.

DEVOTION

Being in agreement as a couple means that you are both walking in agreement in terms of your expectations for the future; acceptance of those expectations invites you both to walk together in love and peace. When a couple is not in agreement of the expectations or hold unrealistic expectations, it drives an invisible wedge between the couple, causing the marriage to be on a path to distrust and doubt. God wants you to walk in agreement as one. Find agreement and clearly define your expectations within the marriage.

Husband READ to Wife: James 4:12

There is one Lawgiver, who is able to save and to destroy. Who are you to judge another?

Wife READ to Husband: Matthew 7:1-2

Judge not, that you be not judged. For with what judgment you judge, you will be judged; and with the measure you use, it will be measured back to you.

MARRIAGE CHALLENGE

What does your spouse do that makes your life easier, fuller, and more satisfying? Tell them. (If you've told them before… tell them again)

Pastor's Sausage and Potato Soup with Kale

Remember to follow this recipe to the letter. It's not about the meal; it's about the *priority time* that you spend together.

Ingredients:
3 thick slices diced turkey bacon
3 tbsp butter (or margarine)
1 large chopped onion
1 cup sliced carrots
1/4 tsp dried leaf thyme
1 BIG tight Hug (Use this hug earlier in the recipe to set the tone)
1 clove garlic, finely minced
1/4 cup whole wheat flour
4 cups chicken broth
4 large fresh Italian chicken sausages, cooked, diced
4 cups diced potatoes
1 1/2 to 2 cups chopped kale, fresh or frozen
2 tbsp chopped parsley
1 cup heavy cream
5 generous cups of love (feel free to use more if you feel the need)
salt and freshly ground black pepper, to taste
    (but don't be surprised if you don't need it)

Directions:
HUG. Cook the bacon in a large saucepan until browned (not quite crispy); remove to paper towels to drain off the grease. Hug. Drain off some of the bacon drippings, leaving a few tsp in the pan. Hug. Add butter to the pan, along with the onions and carrots. Hug. Cook, stirring until the onions are good and tender. Add the thyme and garlic and continue cooking, stirring, for 1 minute longer. Stir in love, Add the flour and cook, stirring, until the flour is well mixed.

Hug. Add the chicken broth and bring to a boil, stirring frequently. Cover, reduce heat, and simmer for about 10 minutes. Add the diced sausage and potatoes; cover and cook for 15 minutes longer. Hug. Add the kale; cover and cook for 5 to 10 minutes, or until vegetables are very tender. Add the cream and the bacon. Taste and add salt and pepper, as needed. Heat through and serve. (did you bring enough hugs?) Top this delicious soup with a little cheese (for me this is the secret ingredient...oh.. don't forget to Hug).

Day Ten Challenge Reflection

The Pastor Chef Challenge is 40 days of praying together, reading together, and cooking together. Close the day with a *Family Declaration!* Reflect on your prayers and praise God for the day.

Praise Report:

_____

_____

_____

_____

How does today's scripture apply to your family?

_____

_____

_____

_____

How was the meal? Did you make any changes (write it down)

_____

_____

_____

_____

What is God saying to you?

_____

_____

CHALLENGE DAY ELEVEN

pray without ceasing.
1 Thessalonians 5:17

Turn your entire life into an opportunity to pray. Whether it's a big event or situation or one of the small and mundane parts of your day, turn it into an excuse, or should we call it, an opportunity to pray to a God that never loses interest in your life. Every thought, every action, every moment, every decision, every corner of your life and every corner of your marriage should become an opportunity to pray. Before you get out of bed, pray, once you get out of bed, pray, before you brush your teeth, pray, and then comes the spicy parts of your day. Trust God enough to talk to Him about everything. Pray without ceasing.

DAILY PRAYER

Before you start your day, before you leave your room in the morning, hold hands and PRAY:
Lord, thank You for teaching us how to walk with You. Thank You, Lord, for guiding and directing us as we walk hand in hand only in the directions that You lead us. If ever we find ourselves moving in the wrong direction, we trust you, Lord, to redirect our family and change our path. We commit to living out our marriage one step at a time trusting You to be our guide and direct our steps. Lord, we may not know exactly where we are going, but we trust You and that is enough for us. AMEN.

DEVOTION

Nothing is too hard for God. Nothing is out of His reach. No marriage is too boring that He can't add a little joy. No marriage is so disconnected that God can't open lines of communication for you to connect. No marriage is so dead that God can't restore and revive and bring life to what others thought was impossible. In fact, it's doing the impossible that brings God the most glory. All it takes is trusting God with your marriage and being sensitive to the needs of your spouse and surrendering your will to His will.

Husband READ to Wife: 1 Peter 3:7

Husbands, likewise, dwell with them with understanding, giving honor to the wife, as to the weaker vessel, and as being heirs together of the grace of life, that your prayers may not be hindered.

Wife READ to Husband: Romans 12:9-11

Let love be without hypocrisy. Abhor what is evil. Cling to what is good. Be kindly affectionate to one another with brotherly love, in honor giving preference to one another; not lagging in diligence, fervent in spirit, serving the Lord;

MARRIAGE CHALLENGE

If you have children tell them how wonderful your spouse is, if you don't: Phone a friend.

Pastor Chefs Batter-Fried Eggplant Chips

Remember to follow this recipe to the letter. It's not about the meal; it's about the *priority time* that you spend together.

Ingredients:
2 large eggplants
1/4 tsp salt
1/2 cup vegetable oil, for frying
2 cups flour
1/2 tsp baking powder
1 tsp ground cumin
1 infectious smile
   (this means that you *refuse* to stop smiling till your spouse joins you)
1 tsp ground coriander
1 tsp paprika
1/2 tsp red pepper flakes
A gob of love and grace (a gob is a lot)
1 1/2 cups water
1 tbsp vegetable oil
1 tbsp of comfort

Directions:

Wash the eggplants and cut them into 1/2 to 1-inch slices. Place them in a bowl and sprinkle them with the salt, and allow them to sit for at least 15 minutes (hug one another the entire 15 minutes while you wait) to render some of their liquid and bitterness. (Don't skip this step)

Heat the oil for frying in a heavy skillet over high heat and prepare a batter by mixing together the remaining ingredients. Pray.

When ready to fry, drop the eggplant slices, a few at a time, into the batter, making sure that they are well coated, and fry, turning once, for 3 to 5 minutes on each side. Drain on paper towel and sprinkle with a dash more of salt. Serve hot.

**Feed chips to each other and smile at one another,
smiling is infectious and comforting.**

Day Eleven Challenge Reflection

The Pastor Chef Challenge is 40 days of praying together, reading together, and cooking together. Close the day with a *Family Declaration!* Reflect on your prayers and praise God for the day.

Praise Report:

_____

_____

_____

_____

How does today's scripture apply to your family?

_____

_____

_____

How was the meal? Did you make any changes (write it down)

_____

_____

_____

What is God saying to you?

_____

_____

CHALLENGE DAY TWELVE

However, this kind does not go out except by prayer and fasting.
Matthew 17:21

The entire Pastor Chef concept came after 40 days of fasting, prayer, and personal marital commitment. We discovered that sometimes some issues required a little extra effort. Some issues require a little more passion and commitment than simply being on your knees in prayer. Fasting moves your prayers to an entirely different level of power and passion. It takes a great deal of patience and endurance, but real fasting has a way of elevating your prayer life to a point where God can move in ways that normal, passive prayer can never match. There is real power in the prayer of agreement. Can you imagine the levels of power that a married couple could have if they were willing to FAST in agreement? Give it a try, watch God move.

DAILY PRAYER

Before you start your day, before you leave your room in the morning, hold hands and PRAY:

Lord, grow us up in the knowledge and power of prayer and fasting. As we reach out to pray with and for others, give us ever-lasting faith to believe and trust You, Lord, for the answers. Lord, we KNOW that with You absolutely nothing is impossible. Your Word not only expresses that directly but illustrates it over and over again. Help us, Lord, to have faith enough to move the mountains in our marriage. AMEN.

DEVOTION

It is a husband *and* a wife that mutually complete one another, giving the world God's complete picture of oneness that God intended for the world to see in marriage. God wants to reveal His unconditional love to the world through your marriage. He wants the world to see forgiveness, passion, commitment, and unity within your marriage. By maintaining a Godly relationship, you have the opportunity to show the world what God looks like.

Challenge Day Twelve Declaration

We declare and decree that marriage is marked by our ability to speak love into one another and not confusion. We use our words to bless and not harm. We speak favor and victory over our family, friends, and loved ones. We DECLARE victory. We DECLARE peace in the storm. We DECLARE that our family is talented, beautiful, and blessed beyond measure.

Husband READ to Wife: John 17:22-23

And the glory which You gave Me I have given them, that they may be one just as We are one: I in them, and You in Me; that they may be made perfect in one, and that the world may know that You have sent Me, and have loved them as You have loved Me.

Wife READ to Husband: Matthew 19:6

So then, they are no longer two but one flesh. Therefore what God has joined together, let not man separate.

MARRIAGE CHALLENGE

In front of a mirror (with no one around but you and your spouse), renew your vows and reminisce about how you felt the first time you took them (enjoy this moment).

Pastor Chefs Chicken with Mango Chutney

CHALLENGE DAY 12
PASTOR CHEFS
RECIPE
(COOK TOGETHER)

Remember to follow this recipe to the letter. It's not about the meal; it's about the *priority time* that you spend together.

Ingredients:
1 lb. boneless, skinless chicken breasts
3/4 cup frozen mangoes (or fresh)
1 tbsp pure maple syrup or honey
1 full kiss (give your honey some sugar)
½ apple
½ onion
1½ cups water
2 tbsp olive oil
2 tbsp raisins
1 tbsp brown sugar
1 full measure of Faith
1 tbsp red pepper
2 tbsp cider vinegar
1 tbsp lime juice
1 tbsp mustard seed
2 tbsp curry powder
1 tbsp garlic powder
1 tbsp chili powder
½ tsp. salt
Black pepper (to taste)

Directions:
Dice all fruits and vegetables. Once done, kiss your spouse and hold that kiss for as long as you can. Pray. Bring water to a boil in a large pot. Pray.
Add all ingredients except chicken.

Reduce heat to simmer. Cook for 30-40 minutes, stirring occasionally. Reduce sauce to syrup-like consistency. While simmering, take this entire time to snuggle up on the sofa (don't give up, don't move, just snuggle till the simmering is done) Heat a non-stick pan to medium. Cut chicken into 4 oz. portions. Cook chicken for 5-6 minutes/side, until no longer pink in center. Let chicken rest for about 5 minutes … do NOT slice into it or you'll release the juices and dry it out (this might take a little patience, use it). Top each chicken breast with a couple scoops of the mango chutney (top each dish with prayer).

Day Twelve Challenge Reflection

The Pastor Chef Challenge is 40 days of praying together, reading together, and cooking together. Close the day with a *Family Declaration!* Reflect on your prayers and praise God for the day.

Praise Report:

_____

_____

_____

_____

How does today's scripture apply to your family?

_____

_____

_____

How was the meal? Did you make any changes (write it down)

_____

_____

_____

_____

What is God saying to you?

_____

_____

CHALLENGE DAY THIRTEEN

His lord said to him, 'Well done, good and faithful servant; you have been faithful over a few things, I will make you ruler over many things. Enter into the joy of your lord.'
Matthew 25:23

Don't just pray about it, be about it. How many of your prayers could you see answered if you just got up and worked on them? How many of your prayers are actually well within your power to achieve but you refuse to act because of fear and doubt. God may not be responding to your prayers because He's already giving you the power and the ability to achieve the very prayer you're standing on. Is it possible that God will not do for you, what you can so easily do for yourself? We give God the glory and the honor when we do what we can do, and seek God to do the things that we cannot. God is able, and so are you.

DAILY PRAYER

Before you start your day, before you leave your room in the morning, hold hands and PRAY:
Lord, we trust You and refuse to lean on our own understanding. We trust You with ALL of our heart. We acknowledge You in all our ways and all that we do. We ask You to direct our path. Lord, please order our steps and take full charge of our lives and direction. Help us to do all that we need to do to please You and strengthen our marriage. AMEN.

DEVOTION

Marriages are so much stronger when both partners are looking for ways to please and serve each other. Jesus revealed to us the proper attitude we should have when he stripped himself of His clothing and bowed down to wash the feet of His disciples. When we truly put the needs of our spouses first, our actions and how we use our time and our daily choices will reflect those values, and our spouses will be much more likely to want to do the same. Loving your spouse by serving your spouse will transform your relationship and renew your marriage.

Challenge Day Thirteen Declaration

We declare and decree that our marriage will not be a place where fear resides. Our marriage is a place where we have good thoughts not thoughts of defeat or loss. By faith, we are able, we are strong, we are anointed, we are equipped, and we are empowered! Our thoughts are guided by an active God who's Word we keep in our hearts. No obstacle can defeat us, because our minds are focused on victory.

Husband READ to Wife: Galatians 6:7-8

Do not be deceived, God is not mocked; for whatever a man sows, that he will also reap. For he who sows to his flesh will of the flesh reap corruption, but he who sows to the Spirit will of the Spirit reap everlasting life.

Wife READ to Husband: Galatians 6:9-10

And let us not grow weary while doing good, for in due season we shall reap if we do not lose heart. Therefore, as we have opportunity, let us do good to all, especially to those who are of the household of faith.

MARRIAGE CHALLENGE

Write a love letter to your spouse. (A REAL love letter put some thought into it).

Pastor Chefs Crispy Crab Cakes

Remember to follow this recipe to the letter. It's not about the meal; it's about the *priority time* that you spend together.

Ingredients:
1 tbsp plus 2 tsp extra-virgin olive oil
2 scallions, thinly sliced
½ cup finely chopped red bell pepper
1 cup panko (Japanese breadcrumbs)
1 large egg, lightly beaten
2 tbsp nonfat milk
1 tsp Worcestershire sauce
2 tbsp dijon mustard (Pastor Bill LOVES dijon with ANYTHING)
1 tbsp fresh lemon juice, plus lemon wedges for serving
1 *fresh* compliment (one that your spouse has never heard you offer)
½ tsp Old Bay Seasoning
Dash of hot sauce
1 lb lump crab or crab claw meat, picked over
Lay on a thick layer of encouragement
Kosher salt and freshly ground pepper
Olive-oil cooking spray

Directions:
Heat 2 tsp olive oil in a large nonstick skillet over medium-high heat. Compliment your spouse. Add the scallions and bell pepper and cook until they begin to soften, about 2 minutes. Cool slightly.

Mix ½ cup panko, the egg and milk in a small bowl. In a medium bowl, whisk the Worcestershire sauce, mustard, lemon juice, Old Bay and hot sauce; fold in the crabmeat, panko mixture, scallion bell pepper mixture, 1/4 tsp salt and a pinch of pepper. Shape into 8 patties and refrigerate 30 minutes (this looks like a good place to stop and kiss your spouse).

Coat the crab cakes with the remaining ½ cup panko. Pray. Heat the remaining 1 tbsp olive oil in the skillet over medium-high heat. Encourage your spouse, they need it. Mist the crab cakes with cooking spray and cook, sprayed-side down, 3 to 4 minutes. Spray the tops, flip and cook 3 to 4 more minutes. Serve with lemon wedges.

Before you eat, give your spouse 3 *new* compliments.

Day Thirteen Challenge Reflection

**The Pastor Chef Challenge is 40 days of praying together, reading together, and cooking together. Close the day with a *Family Declaration!*
Reflect on your prayers and praise God for the day.**

Praise Report:

_____

_____

_____

_____

How does today's scripture apply to your family?

_____

_____

_____

_____

How was the meal? Did you make any changes (write it down)

_____

_____

_____

_____

What is God saying to you?

_____

_____

CHALLENGE DAY FOURTEEN

Oh, sing to the Lord a new song! Sing to the Lord, all the earth.
Psalms 96:1

If your relationship is becoming routine, shake things up a bit. Move the furniture, cook an exotic dish, ask God for a new song. A lot of couples complain that their marriage has become routine, but then refuse to do anything new to change the tone. God wants His people to keep their worship fresh and new. God also wants us to keep our relationships fresh and new. Make up your mind that you *refuse* to let your marriage become boring. Do something new, shake things up. Let God get the glory from your fresh new perspective within your marriage.

DAILY PRAYER

Before you start your day, before you leave your room in the morning, hold hands and PRAY:
Lord, I pray that as a couple we develop a deeper and more passionate hunger for You. Help us to love You so much that praising and worshiping You becomes a way of life. Oh, Lord, we so desire for Your holiness to permeate our entire lives so that we can live in a way that sets us apart for Your purpose and your plan for our marriage. Help us, Lord, to better focus on You, and let our marriage be a reflection of that focus. AMEN.

DEVOTION

When you and your spouse are emotionally connected and your love banks are full everything seems brighter. When you put in the work to connect with your spouse the whole world looks brighter and you will notice that goals seem easier to accomplish when you're functioning as an anointed team. Pray together. Fast together. Worship together. Watch God move in ways that you did not even think was possible. There is real power in being spiritually connected in your marriage.

Challenge Day Fourteen Declaration

We declare and decree that we will always be sensitive to the emotional needs of our spouse. We declare that together we will lift the fallen, restore the broken, and encourage the discouraged. Our marriage is full of kindness, love and affection. We commit that our marriage will become someone's example of what a Godly marriage should be. We are willing to allow our relationship to become a testimony and an example for others to watch and follow.

Husband READ to Wife: Proverbs 27:19

As in water face reflects face, So a man's heart reveals the man.

Wife READ to Husband: Proverbs 18:2

A fool has no delight in understanding, but in expressing his own heart.

MARRIAGE CHALLENGE

Does the way you spend your time reflect your love for your spouse? If not, why not? Have a real discussion about this with your spouse. Take charge.

Pastor Chefs Five-spice Glazed Salmon

Ingredients:
¼ cup molasses
4 tsp soy sauce
2 cups of laughter
1½ tsp five-spice powder
2 large cloves garlic, minced
1½ lbs salmon fillets
1 tbsp orange zest
Parsley or cilantro for serving

Remember to follow this recipe to the letter. It's not about the meal; it's about the *priority time* that you spend together.

Directions:
In a small bowl, whisk the molasses, soy sauce, five-spice powder, and garlic.

Put the salmon skin side down on a large plate and pour the molasses mixture over it.

Flip the fillets so they are skin side up. Let the fish marinate for 15 minutes at room temperature.

Position a rack 6 inches from the broiler and heat the broiler on high. Tell a joke that makes your spouse laugh out loud. Line a large rimmed baking sheet with parchment paper (or foil coated with cooking spray.)

Arrange the salmon skin side down on the baking sheet. Rub your spouse's back. Brush the salmon with any remaining marinade from the plate.

Broil the salmon for 5-8 minutes until cooked (time will depend on the thickness of your fillet and how well you like your salmon cooked).

Garnish with orange zest and parsley. Serve hot.

While eating dinner, laugh together it makes the heart grow fonder.

Day Fourteen Challenge Reflection

The Pastor Chef Challenge is 40 days of praying together, reading together, and cooking together. Close the day with a *Family Declaration!* Reflect on your prayers and praise God for the day.

Praise Report:

_____

_____

_____

_____

How does today's scripture apply to your family?

_____

_____

_____

_____

How was the meal? Did you make any changes (write it down)

_____

_____

_____

_____

What is God saying to you?

_____

_____

CHALLENGE DAY FIFTEEN

Assuredly, I say to you, whatever you bind on earth will be bound in heaven, and whatever you loose on earth will be loosed in heaven.
Matthew 18:18

The bible is pretty clear when it says that if two of us agree on earth about anything that we ask, it shall be done for them by the Father. God wants us to know and to understand that there is so much power in the ability to pray and seek God's face in unity. Binding our prayers to the Word of God in agreement and love can generate and produce new levels of power in your marriage. The word "bind" means to tie together. This is the same word that would be used to describe your marriage vows. Two becoming one, two voices become one spirit. Trust God, agree, connect, and watch God move.

DAILY PRAYER

Before you start your day, before you leave your room in the morning, hold hands and PRAY:
Oh Mighty Lord, we come to You touching and agreeing that You will bless our family and bring peace and joy into our home. Lord, please allow our hard work and labor to bring not only favor, success, and prosperity, but great emotional fulfillment into our household as well. If the work that we are doing is not in line with Your will, reveal it to us, Lord. Guide us and take us down the right path. We commit to going where ever You lead. AMEN.

DEVOTION

God wants to bless you, but the important question to ask is: are you willing to pay the price for your own blessings? Too many people are sitting around waiting for God to bless them without being willing to honestly pay the price. They pretend to be committed, they pretend to be motivated, they pretend to be obedient and correctable, but in the end, they miss out on God's blessings for their life because God only brings real blessings to real commitment. You can't fool God. Why try?

Challenge Day Fifteen Declaration

We declare and decree that we will put our faith into action. We will not be passive or indifferent towards our relationship. We will demonstrate our faith by taking bold and aggressive steps towards God together. We will not be ashamed to show our faith in God nor our commitment towards one another. God will do AMAZING things for our marriage because we place ALL of our confidence in Him.

Husband READ to Wife: Ecclesiastes 5:10

He who loves silver will not be satisfied with silver; Nor he who loves abundance, with increase. This also is vanity.

Wife READ to Husband: Proverbs 13:11

Wealth gained by dishonesty will be diminished, But he who gathers by labor will increase.

MARRIAGE CHALLENGE

Do you have a dream for your life together? Share your marriage dream with your spouse. Don't leave out the details.

Pastor Chefs Shrimp and Broccoli Stir-Fry

Ingredients:

1 lbs medium shrimp, peeled and deveined
1 tbsp cornstarch
2½ tbsp canola oil, divided
1 lbs of unqualified and unpasteurized joy
¼ cup (1-inch) diagonally cut green onions
2 tsp minced peeled fresh ginger
3 garlic cloves, thinly sliced
2 cups broccoli florets
5 hugs
¼ cup lower-sodium soy sauce
2 tbsp rice vinegar
1 tsp honey
2 BIG sloppy kisses (give your spouse some honey)
1/8 tsp crushed red-pepper

Directions:

Combine shrimp and cornstarch in a medium bowl, tossing to coat. Heat a large wok or skillet over high heat. Kiss your spouse right on the lips while you wait for the pan to heat. Add 1 tbsp oil to pan; swirl to coat Add shrimp mixture, and stir-fry 4 minutes. Pray. Remove shrimp from pan; place in a medium bowl. Add 1½ tsp oil to pan; swirl to coat. Add green onions, ginger, and garlic to pan; stir-fry 45 seconds. Hug. Add onion mixture to shrimp.

Add remaining 1 tbsp oil to pan; swirl to coat. Hug. Add broccoli' stir-fry 1½ minutes. Stir in shrimp mixture, soy sauce, even tighter hug, and remaining ingredients; bring to a boil.

Cook 1 minute or until shrimp are done and broccoli is crisp-tender.

Oh and don't forget to hug again before you sit down for dinner

Remember to follow this recipe to the letter. It's not about the meal; it's about the *priority time* that you spend together.

Day Fifteen Challenge Reflection

The Pastor Chef Challenge is 40 days of praying together, reading together, and cooking together. Close the day with a *Family Declaration!* Reflect on your prayers and praise God for the day.

Praise Report:

_____

_____

_____

_____

How does today's scripture apply to your family?

_____

_____

_____

_____

How was the meal? Did you make any changes (write it down)

_____

_____

_____

_____

What is God saying to you?

_____

_____

CHALLENGE DAY SIXTEEN

*So Jesus stood still and called them, and said, "What do you want
Me to do for you?"*
Matthew 20:32

What exactly do you want God to do for your family? What exactly are you trusting God to see you through? What *exactly* are you praying for? This question seems obvious when you're asking this question to a blind man, but not so obvious to a man on his knees praying for God to move in his family. What *exactly* do you want God to do for you and your family? Do you have the faith to be direct and ask specifically for a blessing, or a promise, or a miracle or a dream that you are convinced God placed in your heart? If you're not even sure what you want God to do, don't you think it's time you sat down with your spouse and came up with a specific game plan and start praying accordingly? There is nothing wrong with being specific, just trust God enough to let Him make adjustments along the way for your greater good.

DAILY PRAYER

Before you start your day, before you leave your room in the morning, hold hands and PRAY:
Lord, we commit our finances to You. Take charge of our finances and use them for Your purpose. May our family be better stewards of all that God has given to us and walk in total agreement with God as to how it is to be disbursed. We pray that You will help us to live free from debt and doubt. Where we have not been wise, we ask for You to bring restoration and guidance. Help us to remember that all we have belongs to You and to be grateful for it. AMEN.

DEVOTION

When you accept the fact that you're blessed by God, anointed by God, and called according to His purpose, you begin to recognize the power that is ever present within you. When you learn to love yourself and recognize yourself to be a mighty person of God, you learn to set boundaries that honor not only the God in you, but the person you are meant to be. Once you learn to respect yourself, you're better able to be a good steward of the many gifts God has placed within you.

We declare and decree that breakthroughs are coming for our family, sudden burst of spiritual power and goodness are coming to our family. Not a trickle, not a stream, but a flood of anointing and energy is coming to our family; a flood of healing, a flood of favor, a flood of wisdom, and a flood of finances are all coming to our family. We are a family marked by blessings and deliverance. His love and kindness towards our family will become a testimony for others of just how good our God can be.

{ 74 }

Husband READ to Wife: Ephesians 5:28

In this same way, husbands ought to love their wives as their own bodies. He who loves his wife loves himself.

Wife READ to Husband: Romans 12:1

Therefore, I urge you, brothers, in view of God's mercy, to offer your bodies as living sacrifices, holy and pleasing to God--this is your spiritual act of worship.

MARRIAGE CHALLENGE

Speak to your spouse more kindly than you talk to anyone else in the world. Too often we speak the most harshly to the people who love us the most. Do you do this already? Discuss.

Pastor Chefs Turkey Sausage and Spinach Lasagna

Ingredients:

¼ cup all-purpose flour
1 cup 1% low-fat milk
1 cup unsalted chicken stock
1 tbsp canola oil
1 dab of anointed oil (you might want to anoint your spouse)
1 bay leaf
¼ tsp kosher salt
½ tsp black pepper
Cooking spray
2 tbsp water
1 (12-ounce) package fresh spinach
2 (4-ounce) links hot turkey Italian sausage
½ cup chopped shallots
1 tbsp minced garlic
10 bags of encouragement (you may need more)
6 no-boil lasagna noodles
1½ cups part skim ricotta cheese
1 ounce part—skim mozzarella cheese, shredded (about ¼ cup)
1 ounce fresh Parmesan cheese, grated (about ¼ cup)

Directions:

Preheat oven to 375 degrees.

Weigh or lightly spoon flour into a dry measuring cup; level with a knife. Pray. Combine flour and next 4 ingredients (through bay leaf) in a medium saucepan over medium heat, stirring with a whisk. Cook 8 minutes or until thick and bubbly, stirring frequently. Hug your spouse while you wait. Remove from heat; stir in salt and pepper. Discard bay leaf. Spread 1 cup milk mixture in bottom of an 11 x 7 inch broiler safe glass or ceramic baking dish coated with cooking spray.

Heat a large skillet over medium heat. Add 2 tbsp water and spinach to pan; cook 2 minutes or until spinach wilts. Kiss your spouse on the cheek (just the cheek). Drain spinach, pressing until barely moist. Increase heat to medium-high. Remove casings from sausage. Add sausage to pan; cook 4 minutes or until browned, stirring to crumble. Remove sausage from pan. Add shallots and garlic to pan; sauté 2 minutes. Stir in remaining milk mixture, spinach, and cooked sausage. Remove pan from heat.

Arrange 2 lasagna noodles over milk mixture in baking dish; top with ½ cup ricotta and one-third of spinach mix. Repeat layers twice. Sprinkle with mozzarella and parmesan cheese. Cover with foil coated with cooking spray. Bake at 375 for 40 min. Remove foil.

Preheat broiler to high. Broil 4 minutes or until cheese is golden brown. Let stand 10 min. Hold your spouse in your arms for the entire 10 minutes.

Day Sixteen Challenge Reflection

The Pastor Chef Challenge is 40 days of praying together, reading together, and cooking together. Close the day with a *Family Declaration!* Reflect on your prayers and praise God for the day.

Praise Report:

_____

_____

_____

_____

How does today's scripture apply to your family?

_____

_____

_____

_____

How was the meal? Did you make any changes (write it down)

_____

_____

_____

_____

What is God saying to you?

_____

_____

CHALLENGE DAY SEVENTEEN

The word of the LORD came to me...
Jeremiah 1:4

Do you recognize God's voice when He talks to you? Or, is there too much noise in your life and world to hear from God? If you're having a hard time hearing God's voice; consider going into a time and season of fasting. Allow your time of fasting to silence the noise and various distractions in your life so that you can better hear where God is trying to lead you and your family. The more time you spend in prayer and fasting the better you will be at distinguishing God's voice from your inner (and sometimes selfish) desires. The more you talk to God, the more you're able to recognize His voice in times of trouble. He's talking to you, can you hear Him?

DAILY PRAYER

Before you start your day, before you leave your room in the morning, hold hands and PRAY:
Lord, help us to examine our ways so that we can return to Your ways no matter how far we stray off of Your path. Enable us Lord to take any and every step necessary for us to remain pure before You. We want our marriage to be Holy as You are Holy. We know that You have called us to purity, holiness, and faithfulness. Open our eyes and ears Lord so that we can better see and hear Your wonders and glory in our lives and in our marriage. AMEN.

DEVOTION

When times get hard it's hard to pray let alone praise, but those are the time where it is that much more important for married couples to come together and both PRAY and PRAISE God together. Every marriage has hard times, but it's during those times of challenge where you get to show your spouse what you're really made of. Do you pray more or work extra hours? Do you pray more or drink more? Do you pray more or exercise more? Do you pray more or do you use your own means of escape. Let your family see what you're made of by leaning on God that much more. It will change the tone in your entire household.

Challenge Day Seventeen Declaration

We declare and decree that there is a special anointing of peace over our family. God is going to move obstacles that block our peace aside and leave calm and peaceful situations in front of us. His yoke is easy and His burden is light, therefore we refuse to accept the struggles and burdens that the world wants to place on us. What has been difficult for us in the past will no longer slow us down. God's favor and anointing is taking the weight completely off our shoulders and removing the pressure of trying to keep up with life.

Husband READ to Wife: Psalms 106:1

Praise the LORD. Give thanks to the LORD, for he is good;
his love endures forever.

Wife READ to Husband: Proverbs 27:2

Let another praise you, and not your own mouth; someone else,
and not your own lips.

MARRIAGE CHALLENGE

What are you thankful for? Make a list of ALL the things you are thankful for. Is your spouse on the list? Share your list.

Pastor Chefs Lemon Pepper Shrimp Scampi

CHALLENGE DAY 17
PASTOR CHEFS
RECIPE
(COOK TOGETHER)

Remember to follow this recipe to the letter. It's not about the meal; it's about the *priority time* that you spend together.

Ingredients:
1 cup uncooked orzo
2 tbsp chopped fresh parsley
1 good joke
½ tsp salt divided
7 tsp unsalted butter, divided
1 full measure of faith
1 ½ lbs peeled and deveined jumbo shrimp
2 tsp minced fresh garlic
2 tbsp fresh lemon juice\
¼ tsp freshly ground black pepper

Directions:
Cook orzo according to package directions, omitting salt and fat. Drain. Kiss. Pray. Combine orzo, parsley, and ¼ tsp salt in a medium bowl; keep warm.

While orzo cooks, melt 1 tbsp butter in a large nonstick skillet over medium-high heat. Sprinkle the shrimp with remaining ¼ tsp salt. Add prayer. Add half of shrimp to pan and sauté 2 minutes or until almost done. Kiss your spouse now. Transfer shrimp to a plate. Melt 1 tsp butter in pan. Add remaining shrimp to pan; sauté 2 minutes or until almost done. Transfer shrimp to plate

Melt remaining 1 tbsp butter in pan. Add garlic to pan; cook 30 seconds, stirring constantly. Add shrimp, juice, and pepper to pans; cook 1 minute or until shrimp are done.

Hold hands while eating this dish together (yes, through the entire dish)

Day Seventeen Challenge Reflection

The Pastor Chef Challenge is 40 days of praying together, reading together, and cooking together. Close the day with a *Family Declaration!* Reflect on your prayers and praise God for the day.

Praise Report:

_____

_____

_____

_____

How does today's scripture apply to your family?

_____

_____

_____

_____

How was the meal? Did you make any changes (write it down)

_____

_____

_____

_____

What is God saying to you?

_____

_____

CHALLENGE DAY EIGHTEEN

If you abide in Me, and My words abide in you, you will ask what you desire, and it shall be done for you.
John 15:7

Over the years I've discovered that the best way to move into the presence of God is to devote more time and attention into the Word of God. If you're honest, work to get into God's Word, God's Word will not only get into you, but will become a part of you. If you and your spouse devote your time and your attention to gaining and building a personal relationship with God together through His word, you will begin to see God become an active part of your marriage. Letting God become an active part of your marriage will radically change the way you think about your spouse, the way you live in your home, and the way you love your spouse. When God's word is a part of your marriage, miracles happen and your relationship will move to a whole new level.

DAILY PRAYER

Before you start your day, before you leave your room in the morning, hold hands and PRAY:
Lord, You are the author and the very creator of Love. Teach us, Lord, to love each other deeply and passionately, from our hearts. Thank You, Lord, for the love that is growing stronger and stronger each and every day for my spouse. Thank you for the joy and the peace that we share. We pray that our love will be patient and kind, not proud or selfish, but seeking each other. Protect our love, Lord, and keep our marriage strong. We put our hope in You. AMEN.

DEVOTION

Selfishness is a deep well that many married couples find hard to escape. When a married couple fail to remember that they are spiritually one person following a single path and not two people that happen to be walking together, they start the slow painful process of drifting apart and falling outside of God's purpose for their marriage. Only by remaining focused on the spiritual concept of loving your God with all your heart and loving your spouse as one, do you bind the demons of emotional isolation and selfishness.

Challenge Day Eighteen Declaration

We declare and decree that there is a special anointing of peace over our family. God is going to move obstacles that block our peace aside and leave calm and peaceful situations in front of us. His yoke is easy and His burden is light, therefore we refuse to accept the struggles and burdens that the world wants to place on us. What has been difficult for us in the past will no longer slow us down. God's favor and anointing is taking the weight completely off our shoulders and removing the pressure of trying to keep up with life.

Husband READ to Wife: Philippians 2:3-4

Let nothing be done through selfish ambition or conceit, but in lowliness of mind let each esteem others better than himself. Let each of you look out not only for his own interests, but also for the interests of others.

Wife READ to Husband: 2 Corinthians 10:12-13

For we dare not class ourselves or compare ourselves with those who commend themselves. But they, measuring themselves by themselves, and comparing themselves among themselves, are not wise. We, however, will not boast beyond measure, but within the limits of the sphere which God appointed us--a sphere which especially includes you.

MARRIAGE CHALLENGE

What trait most annoys you about your spouse? There is a pretty good chance that your spouse already knows about it. Let it go.

Pastor Chefs Chicken and Sausage Stew

Ingredients:

3 tbsp all purposed flour
2 tbsp olive oil
2 cups chopped onion
1 cup chopped green bell pepper
1 cup chopped celery
1 compliment (yes, it has to be a new one)
¼ tsp dried thyme
4 oz diced chicken andouille sausage
4 garlic cloves, minced
¼ tsp ground red pepper
1 compliment (that your spouse hears all the time)
12 oz skinless boneless chicken thighs, cut into 1-inch pieces
1½ cup lower-sodium marinara sauce (such as Amy's)
1½ cups fat-free lower-sodium chicken broth
½ cup chopped green onions
3 cups hot cooked white rice

Directions:

Heat flour and oil in a Dutch oven over medium-low heat; cook for 5 minutes or until lightly browned, stirring frequently with a whisk. Compliment your spouse. (The new one) Add onion, bell pepper, celery, thyme, sausage, and garlic; increase heat to medium-high, and cook for 5 minutes stirring mixture frequently. Add ground red pepper and chicken; cook for 1 minute. Stir in marinara sauce and chicken broth; bring to a boil, stirring frequently. Compliment your spouse (one they've heard before) Cover, reduce heat, and simmer for 20 minutes or until chicken is tender. Hug the entire time this is simmering. Remove from heat; stir in green onions. Serve over rice.

Before you eat this dish, dim the lights turn on soft music and eat under candle light.

Day Eighteen Challenge Reflection

The Pastor Chef Challenge is 40 days of praying together, reading together, and cooking together. Close the day with a *Family Declaration!* Reflect on your prayers and praise God for the day.

Praise Report:

_____

_____

_____

_____

How does today's scripture apply to your family?

_____

_____

_____

_____

How was the meal? Did you make any changes (write it down)

_____

_____

_____

_____

What is God saying to you?

_____

_____

CHALLENGE DAY NINETEEN

Yet because of his persistence he will rise and give him as many as he needs.
Luke 11:8

Jesus tells a story about a man who would not take no for an answer. He kept knocking on his friend's door until he gets what he came for in the first place. This is a parable about bold determination and prevailing prayer. There are times that you have to press your way in prayer and refuse to let go of your request from God. You need to pray for your family when everything is telling you to quit. You need to pray through the bad time, the drama, the arguments, and the frustration. You need to pray till you see God move. Press your way and pray. PRAY!

DAILY PRAYER

Before you start your day, before you leave your room in the morning, hold hands and PRAY:

Lord, we humbly ask that You keep us united and strong as a couple. May your cords of peace, honor, respect, and love hold us together during times where our marriage is most challenged. As we become more connected to You, Lord, help us to become closer to You and to each other. Help us to honor one another in our thoughts and in our actions. Help us to love each other that much more. AMEN.

DEVOTION

At some point you're going to have to just accept the fact that you and your spouse are different. You see the world differently, you think different, you were probably raised differently. You have two choices; you can either accept your differences or let your differences tear your relationship apart. Don't let it. Trust that God knew what He was doing when He put the two of you together.

Husband READ to Wife: Ephesians 5:33

Nevertheless let each one of you in particular so love his own wife as himself, and let the wife see that she respects her husband.

Wife READ to Husband: Proverbs 27:2

Wives, likewise, be submissive to your own husbands, that even if some do not obey the word, they, without a word, may be won by the conduct of their wives,

MARRIAGE CHALLENGE

Snuggle on the couch (hugging) for *at least* one hour… Challenge is how long can you hold that hug? (2 hours..3 hours... game on!)

Pastor Chefs Sweet Garlic Chicken (Crock Pot)

Ingredients:
4-6 chicken breasts
1 cup packed brown sugar
1 full and emotionally deep kiss (give your spouse a little sugar)
2/3 cup vinegar (I use apple cider vinegar)
¼ cup lemon-lime soda (diet or regular)
1 funny face to make your spouse laugh (make it a good one)
2-3 tbsp minced garlic
2 tbsp soy sauce
1 tsp fresh ground pepper
2 tbsp corn starch
2 tbsp water
Red pepper flakes (optional)

Directions:
Spray slow cooker with non-stick cooking spray. Pray. Place chicken (frozen, thawed or fresh) inside slow cooker. Mix together brown sugar, vinegar, soda, garlic, soy sauce, and pepper together. Pour over chicken. Cook on low for 6 – 8 hours or high for 4 hours. Can you hug your spouse for 6 hours? (1 hour?)

Take chicken pieces out of slow cooker (mine basically fell apart) and pour remaining sauce into saucepan. Place saucepan over high heat. Mix together corn starch and water, pour into saucepan, and mix well. Kiss your spouse. Let sauce come to a boil and boil for 2-3 minutes, or until it starts to thicken and turns into a glaze. Remove from heat and let sit for a minute or two (it will continue to thicken as it cools down).

Sprinkle red pepper flakes on top if desired. This can be served over rice or noodles. I also like it with a baked potato on the side (it's good on top of the potato too).

When you finish this dish… Go back to that LONG hug.

**CHALLENGE DAY 19
PASTOR CHEFS
RECIPE
(COOK TOGETHER)**

Remember to follow this recipe to the letter. It's not about the meal; it's about the *priority time* that you spend together.

Day Nineteen Challenge Reflection

The Pastor Chef Challenge is 40 days of praying together, reading together, and cooking together. Close the day with a *Family Declaration!* Reflect on your prayers and praise God for the day.

Praise Report:

_____

_____

_____

_____

How does today's scripture apply to your family?

_____

_____

_____

_____

How was the meal? Did you make any changes (write it down)

_____

_____

_____

_____

What is God saying to you?

_____

_____

Challenge Day Twenty

...and by the word of their testimony...
Revelation 12:11

When was the last time you listened to another couples testimony about their marriage? When was the last time you heard a story about how God moved a mountain for another couple? When was the last time you felt the urge to applaud God for somebody else's marriage. Testimonies can ignite a fire under your faith in ways you can't begin to imagine. If God did it for them, He can sure do it for you. Trust Him.

DAILY PRAYER

Before you start your day, before you leave your room in the morning, hold hands and PRAY:

Lord, You are worthy of our praise and adoration. We are amazed at how much we are blessed when we praise You. When we glorify Your name. We feel Your strength. We know that You are with us and keep us strong and safe in times of trouble. We want our entire lives and our entire existence to be centered on You. Without You leading us, we would have lives of complication and drought but with You, Lord, we live lives of victory and peace. AMEN.

DEVOTION

Do you have a big enough vision for your marriage? Are you expecting great things for your marriage or are you just winging it and hoping things work out as you go along. God has given us powerful examples of good and holy marriages that transcend the very idea of worldly marriage tied to emotions and romance. Do you see your spouse as God sees your spouse or are you comparing them to some worldly image? Replace your worldly view of marriage with a higher and better model. Choose God's version, ignore the world's.

Challenge Day Twenty Declaration

We declare and decree we *will* live victorious. Our marriage was created by GOD in His very image. We were made to win. God has placed a crown of favor upon our heads. We are royal priests with a heritage and legacy of victory. We are the head and not the tail, above and never beneath. We live with purpose, passion, and praise because we *know* that God has brought us together so that we could live in victory.

Husband READ to Wife: Proverbs 19:14

Houses and riches are an inheritance from fathers, But a prudent wife is from the Lord.

Wife READ to Husband: Ephesians 5:33

Nevertheless let each one of you in particular so love his own wife as himself, and let the wife see that she respects her husband.

MARRIAGE CHALLENGE

Snuggle on the couch (hugging) for at least one hour… Challenge is how long can you hold that hug? (2 hours..3 hours... game on!)

Pastor Chefs Coconut Shrimp

Ingredients:
2 cups vegetable oil
1 cup Panko bread crumbs
1 cup unsweetened shredded coconut
A dash of tenderness
1 lb. medium shrimp, peeled and deveined...
Kosher salt and freshly ground black pepper, to taste
½ cup all-purpose flour
2 large eggs, beaten
Sweet chili sauce, for serving
Kosher salt and freshly ground black pepper, to taste
Kind words (or spicy words… to taste)
½ cup all-purpose flour
2 large eggs, beaten
Sweet chili sauce, for serving

Remember to follow this recipe to the letter. It's not about the meal; it's about the *priority time* that you spend together.

Directions:
Heat vegetable oil in a large skillet or Dutch oven over medium high heat.
In a large bowl, combine Panko bread crumbs and shredded coconut; set aside and give your spouse a kiss (on the cheek, you can offer more after dinner).
Season the shrimp with salt and pepper, to taste. (this would be a good place for those kind words) Working one at a time, dredge shrimp in the flour, dip into the eggs, then dredge in the coconut mixture, pressing to coat. Pray.
Working in batches, add shrimp to the Dutch oven and fry until evenly golden brown and crispy, about 2-3 minutes. Kiss your spouse (again just on the cheek).
Transfer to a paper towel-lined plate.
Serve immediately with sweet chili sauce, if desired.

Feed each other shrimp and follow it by telling each other "I love you" after each bite.

Day Twenty Challenge Reflection

The Pastor Chef Challenge is 40 days of praying together, reading together, and cooking together. Close the day with a *Family Declaration!* Reflect on your prayers and praise God for the day.

Praise Report:

_____

_____

_____

_____

How does today's scripture apply to your family?

_____

_____

_____

_____

How was the meal? Did you make any changes (write it down)

_____

_____

_____

_____

What is God saying to you?

_____

_____

CHALLENGE DAY TWENTY-ONE

Train up a child in the way he should go,
And when he is old he will not depart from it.
Proverbs 22:6

Everyone wants to feel important. Everyone wants to believe that they have value. Everyone wants to be appreciated. You may not realize this but your spouse and your children hunger for your approval and blessing. They need to hear you tell them they are important and that you are proud of them. They need to hear you tell them that you believe God is going to do great things with them. Ask yourself this question: What seeds are you planting into the spirit of your spouse and your children.

DAILY PRAYER

Before you start your day, before you leave your room in the morning, hold hands and PRAY:
Lord, we thank You and we praise You for bringing us together. We ask that You give us the strength and the anointing to enjoy our time together as a couple and as a family. Thank You for rewarding us with the smile of our spouse and the laughter of our children. Thank You for filling our lives and thoughts with joy, peace, and love. Let Your love flow through our family all the days of our lives. AMEN.

DEVOTION

Agape is that special love that is given because the person who is receiving it needs it more than the person who is giving it. God lavishes His love on us regardless of whether we are worthy of this level of love. God gives us a level of anointing and expectation to display this love to the world so that all can see what it means to be a Christian.

Husband READ to Wife: Genesis 2:24

Therefore a man shall leave his father and mother and be joined to his wife, and they shall become one flesh.

Challenge Day Twenty-One Declaration

We declare and decree that we're building and training our children to be GREAT. We declare that we look for opportunities to encourage our children to bring out the best in them and to help them accomplish their dreams. We will speak words of faith and victory, affirming them, approving them, letting them know that they are valued and important. We will call out the seeds of greatness, and cause them to rise higher and become all that God created them to be.

Wife READ to Husband: Luke 9:23

Then He said to them all, "If anyone desires to come after Me, let him deny himself, and take up his cross daily, and follow Me.

MARRIAGE CHALLENGE

Pray for God to help you see what your marriage can become. He has the power to tear down any walls that have been built up and to heal any wound. Trust Him for something great.

Pastor Chefs Mongolian Beef

Ingredients:
2 tbsp lower-sodium soy sauce
1 tsp sugar
1 tsp cornstarch
1 tsp of cheer
2 tsp dry sherry
2 tsp hoisin sauce
1 tsp rice vinegar
1 tsp chili paste with garlic
2 heaping helpings of laughter
¼ tsp salt
2 tsp peanut oil
1 tbsp minced peeled ginger
1 hug (add to taste)
1 tbsp minced fresh garlic
1 lb sirloin steak, thinly sliced across the grain
16 medium green onions, cut into 2-inch pieces

Directions:
Combine first 8 ingredients; stir with a whisk until smooth. Whisk spouse around room (ok, back to recipe).

Heat a large nonstick skillet over medium-high heat. Kiss your spouse. Add oil; swirl to coat. Add ginger, garlic, and beef; sauté 2 minutes or until beef is browned. Tell a joke (pretend to laugh) Add onion; sauté 30 seconds. Add soy sauce mixture; cook 1 minute or until thickened, stirring constantly. Pray.

Dance cheek to cheek before you take your first bite (music is optional)

CHALLENGE DAY 21
PASTOR CHEFS
RECIPE
(COOK TOGETHER)

Remember to follow this recipe to the letter. It's not about the meal; it's about the *priority time* that you spend together.

Day Twenty-One Challenge Reflection

The Pastor Chef Challenge is 40 days of praying together, reading together, and cooking together. Close the day with a *Family Declaration!* Reflect on your prayers and praise God for the day.

Praise Report:

_____

_____

_____

_____

How does today's scripture apply to your family?

_____

_____

_____

_____

How was the meal? Did you make any changes (write it down)

_____

_____

_____

_____

What is God saying to you?

_____

_____

CHALLENGE DAY TWENTY-TWO

Death and life are in the power of the tongue,
And those who love it will eat its fruit.
Proverbs 18:21

The bible declares that there is an enormous amount of power in your words. God has placed a lot of responsibility into the mouths of His people. If you speak life into your children they will live, if you speak death into your children they will die. Maybe not immediately, but slowly and surely they will lose or gain confidence with life by the words you choose to speak into them. This is also true about your spouse. Speak life into your spouse. Watch this grow emotionally and spiritual. Watch them live with more confidence and abundance from your words.

DAILY PRAYER

Before you start your day, before you leave your room in the morning, hold hands and PRAY:

Lord, we thank You and we praise You for keeping us united and strong. Lord, we thank You for Your words of peace, honor, respect, and love that hold us together that we may live our lives as one. We praise You for allowing us to enjoy spiritual connections that come from harmonious conversations that agree with Yours words. We agree with Your word and will work to make our words and lives reflect that agreement. AMEN.

DEVOTION

Marriage requires a lot of give and take. If any couple wants a successful marriage they should always be in a state of reconciliation and spiritual renewal. You can count on there being times where you say the wrong things or disappoint your spouse. The problem will never be the mistakes you make, the problem will be your willingness to do the hard work it takes to allow you both to press forward in unity. Do the work.

Challenge Day Twenty-Two Declaration

We declare and decree that our words have power. We declare that we will only use our words to lift up our family and speak positive words into our future. We will not use our words to discourage our own efforts. We will declare words of favor, deliverance, restoration, and strength into our home. We declare that our God is bigger than our issues, problems, fears, and concerns. We turn our issues over to God, and that's all we have to say about that.

Husband READ to Wife: 1 John 4:9-10

In this the love of God was manifested toward us, that God has sent His only begotten Son into the world, that we might live through Him. In this is love, not that we loved God, but that He loved us and sent His Son to be the propitiation for our sins.

Wife READ to Husband: 1 John 4:11-12

Beloved, if God so loved us, we also ought to love one another. 12 No one has seen God at any time. If we love one another, God abides in us, and His love has been perfected in us.

MARRIAGE CHALLENGE

Send a text message every hour for 12 hours with *one* trait you love about your spouse.

Pastor Chefs Apple Cider Glazed Pork Chops

Remember to follow this recipe to the letter. It's not about the meal; it's about the *priority time* that you spend together.

Ingredients:
3-4 pork chops ~ we use boneless
1 cup apple cider
2 tbsp brown sugar
2 juicy kisses (give your spouse some juicy sugar)
¼ tsp cinnamon
¼ tsp cayenne
Spice things up in the kitchen
1 tbsp cornstarch
1 tbsp cold apple cider

Directions:
Heat cup of apple cider over medium heat. Pray about your marriage. Add brown sugar, cinnamon, and cayenne; juicy kiss. bring to a simmer. In a small bowl, whisk together tbsp each of the cornstarch and cold apple cider. A little extra Patience with your spouse. Add to simmering liquid and stir until thickened. Pray Pour into bowl and set aside.

In same skillet, heat olive oil. Season pork chops if desired with a little salt and pepper. Cook chops for 3 – 4 minutes each side. Pray. Pour apple cider glaze over the top and cover. Reduce heat to low and simmer for 10 – 15 minutes; until chops are cooked through. Tell your spouse what you would want for Christmas if you won the lottery. Stir and flip the chops occasionally to keep the sugars from burning and sticking. Serve with extra glaze for dipping.

One wash, one dry, one wash, one dry… Share with your spouse what your *favorite* chore is around the house… explain why.

Day Twenty-Two Challenge Reflection

The Pastor Chef Challenge is 40 days of praying together, reading together, and cooking together. Close the day with a *Family Declaration!* Reflect on your prayers and praise God for the day.

Praise Report:

_____

_____

_____

_____

How does today's scripture apply to your family?

_____

_____

_____

_____

How was the meal? Did you make any changes (write it down)

_____

_____

_____

_____

What is God saying to you?

_____

_____

CHALLENGE DAY TWENTY-THREE

Nor do they light a lamp and put it under a basket, but on a lampstand, and it gives light to all who are in the house.
Matthew 5:16

Jesus is the light of the word and He lights up those families that come in to a real relationship with Him. When Moses spent time in God's presence, his entire face glowed. Likewise, when you and your family spend time in God's presence and listen to what He has to say to you it will show all over your faces. Your smiles will be infectious. Your spirits will draw others to you and will make people want to connect with you. Let your light shine, let God's love show.

DAILY PRAYER

Before you start your day, before you leave your room in the morning, hold hands and PRAY:
*Lord, we want to be in a **real** relationship with You. We want to be so connected to You that it shows all over our faces. Lord, we want for others to be able to see Your anointing in every aspect of our lives. We don't want our marriage to be consumed by empty religion or false spirituality. Let our lives and our words be a reflection of our faith and trust in You. AMEN.*

DEVOTION

Marriage should be a time of rejoicing and praise. Marriage is not just an agreement for two people to live together and share space. It's a spiritual union and binding covenant where two people become ONE person in the eyes of God. Everything you do within your marriage is a reflection for your worship. Praise God for your marriage. Your praise and your marriage is now a celebration before a mighty God that loves you.

Husband READ to Wife: 1 Thessalonians 5:16-18

Rejoice always, pray without ceasing, in everything give thanks; for this is the will of God in Christ Jesus for you.

Challenge Day Twenty-Three Declaration

We declare and decree that our marriage will last. We will rejoice in our relationship and thrive not just survive. We will prosper and overcome every difficult situation that comes our way. Our marriage will be marked with success that comes from our personal commitment to success. We will never, ever give up on us, no matter how hard things get we will remember that we are living in God's favor. This is our time. This is our moment. We are blessed.

Wife READ to Husband: Philippians 4:4

Rejoice in the Lord always. Again I will say, rejoice!

MARRIAGE TIPS

Don't put yourself in places of temptation. Put your energy into the one you vowed to love.

Pastor Chefs Burrito Bowl with Creamy Chipotle Sauce

Remember to follow this recipe to the letter. It's not about the meal; it's about the *priority time* that you spend together.

Ingredients:

1 cup uncooked rice or quinoa
1/2 cup salsa (restaurant-style, or your favorite store-bought brand)
1 can black beans, rinsed and drained
1 half of a prayer (per spouse)
2-3 roma tomatoes, diced
1 1/2 cups corn (I use frozen corn, thawed)
Romaine lettuce, chopped
1 half of a hug (per spouse)
Creamy chipotle sauce
Other additions: onion, green onion, bell pepper, avocado, cheese, cilantro

Directions:

Cook rice. (For firmer rice, use 1 cup rice + 1¼ cup water.) Hug... (to taste)

While rice is cooking, pray and then prep your veggies and make the creamy chipotle sauce.

When rice is cooked, stir in salsa while your spouse sings (any song, have fun with this).

Begin layering your bowl: start with rice, then with prayer, then black beans, and vegetables.

Drizzle with a little love and the creamy chipotle sauce on top and enjoy.

Turn off all the lights in the house, enjoy your meal by the light of your relationship (seriously, cut the lights off).

Day Twenty-Three Challenge Reflection

The Pastor Chef Challenge is 40 days of praying together, reading together, and cooking together. Close the day with a *Family Declaration!* Reflect on your prayers and praise God for the day.

Praise Report:

_____

_____

_____

_____

How does today's scripture apply to your family?

_____

_____

_____

_____

How was the meal? Did you make any changes (write it down)

_____

_____

_____

_____

What is God saying to you?

_____

_____

Challenge Day Twenty-Four

Finally, brethren, whatever things are true, whatever things are noble, whatever things are just, whatever things are pure, whatever things are lovely, whatever things are of good report, if there is any virtue and if there is anything praiseworthy—meditate on these things.

Philippians 4:8

It's hard to enjoy life while you're being negative. It's hard to see positive in your life and in your marriage when your entire focus is on the things that are going wrong. Viewing each day with positive expectations and energy is one of the true principles of godly and spiritual happiness and joy. Your behavior is a direct reflection of what you truly believe. If you want a positive life, begin thinking positive thoughts about your life. If you want a positive marriage, begin thinking positive thoughts about your marriage. Find time to get together with your spouse and discuss all of the things in your life that you're really happy about. Think on those things.

DAILY PRAYER

Before you start your day, before you leave your room in the morning, hold hands and PRAY:

Lord, please forgive us when our choices don't line up with our beliefs. Help us to nurture Your Words in our hearts so that we can grow as a couple with maturity and anointing. Teach us Your ways and give us understanding and direction. Allow the values of our faith to affect every single area and aspect of our relationship. Help us to stay committed to living what we believe. Help us to be a real example of a couple that walks by faith and not by sight. AMEN.

DEVOTION

The very best way to be a grace-filled, loving and anointed spouse is to be a praying, loving and accepting spouse. When you get out of the way and let God take the lead in your marriages you begin to see true and lasting results in your relationships. Marriage is not easy, and prayer alone is not a magic bullet, but when you combine your prayers with sincere commitment and action, you begin to see God move in your relationship in ways that you never thought possible. Talk to God, and then do what He says. That's just plain good advice.

Challenge Day Twenty-Four Declaration

We declare and decree that our marriage will be ruled by our faith and not by our fears. We will lean on Your Word and gain confidence by Your spirit. We will meditate on the positive things in our lives and not dwell on the negative. We refuse to worry, but will lift each other up with our words of faith and encouragement. Our minds will stay on what God says about our marriage. God has a plan of success, victory, and abundance for us. We accept His plan.

{ 106 }

Husband READ to Wife: Philippians 1:6

being confident of this very thing, that He who has begun a good work in you will complete it until the day of Jesus Christ;

Wife READ to Husband: Ephesians 2:20

having been built on the foundation of the apostles and prophets, Jesus Christ Himself being the chief corner stone,

MARRIAGE TIPS

Share a song. What is your spouse's favorite song? Play it and then sing it (no it doesn't have to be all that good, just be willing to try).

Pastor Chefs Burrito Seafood Jambalaya

Ingredients:
1 tbsp olive oil
1 onion, chopped
2 celery stalks, sliced
1 green or red pepper, seeded and cut into strips
2 garlic cloves, crushed
1 tsp ground ginger
½ tsp cayenne pepper
1 tsp mild chili powder
1 cup long-grain white rice
2 cups hot chicken broth
1 can (14 oz) chopped tomatoes
3 tbsp coarsely chopped parsley
½ lbs large raw shrimp, peeled and deveined
½ lbs skinned salmon fillet, cut into 1-inch cubes
Dash hot red pepper sauce (optional) we use red pepper flakes
Salt and pepper

Directions:
Heat the oil in a large wide pan over medium heat. Add the onion and cook, stirring, for about 3 minutes. Hug your spouse; add the celery, green or red pepper, garlic, ginger, cayenne, chili powder, and rice, and cook, stirring for 2 minutes.

Pour in the hot broth and stir well, then reduce the heat so that the broth is simmering gently. Cover the pan with a tight fitting lid and simmer for 15 minutes. (Hug your spouse the entire 15 minutes).

Stir in the chopped tomatoes with their juice and 2 tbsp of the parsley, then add the shrimp and salmon. Cover again, and simmer until the seafood is just cooked and the rice has absorbed most of the liquid and is tender, about 3 to 4 minutes.

Add the hot sauce, if using, and season lightly with salt and pepper. Sprinkle with the remaining 1 tbsp parsley and serve hot.

Write a song for your spouse and then sing it!
(it doesn't matter if you have a great voice, sing it anyway)

Remember to follow this recipe to the letter. It's not about the meal; it's about the *priority time* that you spend together.

Day Twenty-Four Challenge Reflection

The Pastor Chef Challenge is 40 days of praying together, reading together, and cooking together. Close the day with a *Family Declaration!* Reflect on your prayers and praise God for the day.

Praise Report:

_____

_____

_____

_____

How does today's scripture apply to your family?

_____

_____

_____

_____

How was the meal? Did you make any changes (write it down)

_____

_____

_____

_____

What is God saying to you?

_____

_____

CHALLENGE DAY TWENTY-FIVE

As iron sharpens iron, So a man sharpens the countenance of his friend.
Proverbs 27:17

If you want to do something great for God, then don't associate with people who are doing nothing! You may have to drastically change your world and relationships, if you want to move in what God has called you to do. Spend time with people who are also living for a purpose. Spend time with people who have ambition and who are pursuing goals. Iron does sharpen Iron and positive ambitious aggressive people who are living to please God will bring out the best in you as well. Don't forget that you get to choose who your friends are; Choose your friends wisely.

DAILY PRAYER

Before you start your day, before you leave your room in the morning, hold hands and PRAY:
Thank You, Lord, that every family is important to You. Thank You, Lord, for allowing me to praise. You've done so much for our family that all I want to do is praise You. You give us strength and breath. You meet all our needs with abundance. You have blessed us with a beautiful family. Lord, You are great! All we want to do is praise You! Hallelujah! AMEN.

DEVOTION

Philippians 4:6 says that we should worry about nothing and pray about everything. When God created marriage He brought two people together to be a power team that can function in such power and agreement that they will be able to overcome every obstacle. Make up your mind that you will trust God more than you will worry about your issues. Trust God over your finances. Trust God over your relationships. Trust God over your fears. Trust God and don't worry. Pray about it and then let it go. (Really… let it go)

Husband READ to Wife: Philippians 4:6

Be anxious for nothing, but in everything by prayer and supplication, with thanksgiving, let your requests be made known to God.

Wife READ to Husband: 1 Peter 5:7

Casting all your care upon Him, for He cares for you.

MARRIAGE TIPS

Make an agreement with your spouse to remind each other not to worry about money, employment or family issues. (You have to be in agreement to trust God).

Pastor Chefs Southern Oven-Fried Chicken

Ingredients:
1 cup (16 tbsp) corn flake crumbs
1 oz of tender loving care
   (just an ounce, too much will keep you from cooking all together)
1 tsp paprika
½ tsp garlic powder
1/4 tsp ground thyme
1 full cup of quality time (as you can squeeze into the dish)
1/4 tsp red pepper
6 halved, skinned chicken breasts
1/4 cup (4 tbsp) low fat buttermilk
1 dash vegetable cooking spray

Remember to follow this recipe to the letter. It's not about the meal; it's about the *priority time* that you spend together.

Directions:
Combine corn flake crumbs and seasonings in a plastic bag, mixing well.

Brush both sides of chicken breasts with buttermilk, place chicken in bag with crumb mixture, shaking to coat. Hold hand and shake together. Shake some more… kiss your spouse… shake it again. (ok, that's enough shaking)

Place chicken on a broiler pan coated with cooking spray, bake, uncovered, at 400°F for 45 minutes or until done. Hold your spouse in your arms… look into each other's eyes for as long as you can without forgetting the chicken is cooking.

Play truth of dare with your spouse while you enjoy your meal.

Day Twenty-Five Challenge Reflection

The Pastor Chef Challenge is 40 days of praying together, reading together, and cooking together. Close the day with a *Family Declaration!* Reflect on your prayers and praise God for the day.

Praise Report:

_____

_____

_____

_____

How does today's scripture apply to your family?

_____

_____

_____

_____

How was the meal? Did you make any changes (write it down)

_____

_____

_____

_____

What is God saying to you?

_____

_____

CHALLENGE DAY TWENTY-SIX

There are many plans in a man's heart, Nevertheless the Lord's counsel—that will stand.
Proverbs 19:21

What is God's plan for your marriage? If you know, great! But, if you're not sure, then take some time and seek God's plan for your relationship. Stay passionate for God's purpose. Make up your mind that you will be complete and on fire for the Lord. Pursue His purpose for your marriage with every ounce of energy that you can muster. There is nothing on earth that can be more satisfying than finding and following God's direction for your marriage. When you're working together to find your purpose you will notice a unity and peace in your relationship that never existed before. Seek God's purpose.

DAILY PRAYER

Before you start your day, before you leave your room in the morning, hold hands and PRAY:
Lord, we seek your direction to know how to pray in every situation and for every concern or issue. Make us bold enough to ask. Enable us to ask according to Your will. Give us faith to believe that impossible things can happen when we pray. Forgive us when we doubt. Replace our doubt with enough faith that we can accept that all things are possible regardless of what we see, because we trust you. AMEN.

DEVOTION

Even the best marriages have hard times. Even the best relationships have difficult moments. Even the most loving couples have arguments. We tend to relish the happy moment and pretend the ugly ones don't even exist. When we learn to trust that sometimes God will hide his most beautiful treasures inside of our ugly moments we begin to find the true joy that comes from a lasting and loving marriage. It's in the rough times that we learn to lean on God and trust each other. A threefold cord is not easily broken. Go ahead weave God into the drama, watch it turn into treasure.

Challenge Day Twenty-Six Declaration

We declare and decree that we are trusting God for BIG things to come into our marriage. We are praying BOLD prayers in complete agreement that God can and will do BIG things for our marriage. We refuse to listen to the people in our lives who cannot see with the eyes of faith and now we choose to see only what God wants us to see. We no longer accept failure as an option. We no longer accept lack as a place. We no longer accept anyone's assessment of our marriage or our relationship that cannot see what God has done or what God is doing in our marriage. There is nothing too difficult for God. We trust Him for the BIG things.

Husband READ to Wife: Matthew 6:28-34

So why do you worry about clothing? Consider the lilies of the field, how they grow: they neither toil nor spin; and yet I say to you that even Solomon in all his glory was not arrayed like one of these. Now if God so clothes the grass of the field, which today is, and tomorrow is thrown into the oven, will He not much more clothe you, O you of little faith? Therefore do not worry, saying, 'What shall we eat?' or 'What shall we drink?' or 'What shall we wear?' For after all these things the Gentiles seek. For your heavenly Father knows that you need all these things. But seek first the kingdom of God and His righteousness, and all these things shall be added to you. Therefore do not worry about tomorrow, for tomorrow will worry about its own things. Sufficient for the day is its own trouble.

Wife READ to Husband: Psalms 126:5-6

Those who sow in tears Shall reap in joy. He who continually goes forth weeping, Bearing seed for sowing, Shall doubtless come again with rejoicing, Bringing his sheaves with him.

Pastor Chefs Taco Pie

Ingredients:
1/4 cup butter
2/3 cup milk
2 pecks on the cheek
1 package taco seasoning mix
2½ cups mashed potato flakes
   (you could also use leftover mashed potatoes and omit the butter and milk)
1 full and emotionally passionate kiss
1 lb ground beef
½ cup chopped onion
½ cup salsa
2 unexpected compliments
1 cup shredded lettuce
1 heaping helping of love and peace
1 medium tomato, chopped
1 cup sharp cheddar cheese, shredded
Sour cream, optional

Directions:
Preheat oven to 350 degrees. Pray for your spouse. In a medium sauce pan, melt butter. Add milk and 2 tbsp taco seasoning. Kiss your spouse on the cheek. Remove from heat and add potato flakes until incorporated. Press mixture into the bottom of a 10-inch pan.

Bake for 7-10 minutes until it just BARELY turns golden brown. Barely kiss your spouse (yes, I said barely… now go for it).

In a medium skillet, cook beef and onions until beef is browned and cooked through. Drain. Hug. Add salsa and remaining taco seasoning. Cook until bubbly.

Pour into crust and then bake for 15 minutes, or until crust is golden brown. Give your spouse a tight loving hug.

Let cool for 5 minutes. Top with cheese, lettuce, and tomatoes. Cut and serve with sour cream if you are one of those who like spoiled cream.

CHALLENGE DAY 26
PASTOR CHEFS
RECIPE
(COOK TOGETHER)

Remember to follow this recipe to the letter. It's not about the meal; it's about the *priority time* that you spend together.

Day Twenty-Six Challenge Reflection

The Pastor Chef Challenge is 40 days of praying together, reading together, and cooking together. Close the day with a *Family Declaration!* Reflect on your prayers and praise God for the day.

Praise Report:

_____

_____

_____

_____

How does today's scripture apply to your family?

_____

_____

_____

_____

How was the meal? Did you make any changes (write it down)

_____

_____

_____

_____

What is God saying to you?

_____

_____

CHALLENGE DAY TWENTY-SEVEN

A man will be satisfied with good by the fruit of his mouth, And the recompense of a man's hands will be rendered to him.
Proverbs 12:14

It's amazing how peaceful and satisfying your life becomes when the words you speak are as sweet as fruit. When you let God be the guide of your words and your words become not only the way you convey information but the way you convey the sweetness of God into the life of your family. A man can be satisfied with good from the fruit (sweet words) of their mouth. If you want peace in your household, try using more peaceful words. You will be surprised by how gentle your home becomes when your words become a reflection of your love and confidence in God.

DAILY PRAYER

Before you start your day, before you leave your room in the morning, hold hands and PRAY:
Lord, help us to become people that only use words that build up and not tear down. Help us, Lord, to speak life into every situation and person in our family and in our lives. Fill us, O' Lord, with the Holy Spirit and an anointing that will sweeten our words with a love, joy and peace that will brighten the hearts of others. Lord, please let the words of our mouth and the meditation of our hearts be acceptable in Your sight, O Lord, You are our redeemer! AMEN.

DEVOTION

Did you marry Prince Charming? Did you marry the magical princess whose love is unconditional and never sees wrong in your behavior? Everyone is looking to marry their fantasy person believing that if they do, they will live happily ever after. However, marriage is not a fantasy and even if you do marry your perfect person, if you don't put in the work to maintain a healthy relationship, you will soon notice that your perfect person is, well, just a person. Spend less time trying to find (or demand your spouse become) the perfect person, and spend more time fighting to *become* the perfect person for your spouse.

Challenge Day Twenty-Seven Declaration

We declare and decree no matter what we are facing God is working things out for our good. He has a plan and a purpose for everything that we are going through. There may be things going on that we don't understand but we refuse to worry. We know that God knows what He's doing and will pull it all together in the end. This is only the beginning and we trust that God has already prepared the end to work in our favor. God's plans are greater than our own, if we trust Him. In the end, our blessings will be amazing!

Husband READ to Wife: Jeremiah 1:4-5

Then the word of the Lord came to me, saying: "Before I formed you in the womb I knew you; Before you were born I sanctified you; I ordained you a prophet to the nations."

Wife READ to Husband: Ephesians 2:10

For we are His workmanship, created in Christ Jesus for good works, which God prepared beforehand that we should walk in them.

MARRIAGE TIPS

Read 1 Corinthians 13, the love chapter, to refresh your memories as to what love is supposed to look like. Discuss.

Pastor Chefs Creamy Crock-pot Chicken and Broccoli Over Rice

Remember to follow this recipe to the letter. It's not about the meal; it's about the *priority time* that you spend together.

Ingredients:
3-4 boneless chicken breasts
1 10 oz can cream of chicken soup
1 10 oz can cheddar soup
1 14 oz can chicken broth
½ tsp of pleasant words (just roll with this)
½ tsp salt
¼ tsp garlic salt seasoning
1 cup of tickles
    (don't go overboard with this one.. it can ruin the meal if you use to much)
1 cup sour cream
1 tbsp of laughter
6 cups broccoli florets, just fork tender
    (I cook it in boiling water for 3-4 minutes)
1 cup shredded cheddar cheese

Directions:
Place soups, chicken broth, salt, and garlic seasoning into a crock-pot over low heat. Tell a joke. Whisk until smooth. Pray. Place chicken in, pressing to the bottom. Kiss your spouse. Cover lid and cook on low for 6 hours or on high for 3 hours.

When chicken is cooked, use 2 forks to shred into bite size pieces. Stir in sour cream and broccoli.

Feed one another (until it's all gone).

Day Twenty-Seven Challenge Reflection

The Pastor Chef Challenge is 40 days of praying together, reading together, and cooking together. Close the day with a *Family Declaration!* Reflect on your prayers and praise God for the day.

Praise Report:

_____

_____

_____

_____

How does today's scripture apply to your family?

_____

_____

_____

_____

How was the meal? Did you make any changes (write it down)

_____

_____

_____

_____

What is God saying to you?

_____

_____

Challenge Day Twenty-Eight

This is My commandment, that you love one another as I have loved you.
John 15:12

Love is not really a choice. It is a command from God that we love one another. The expectations within a marriage move to a whole new level of expectation. You are still commanded to love but now you're commanded to love your spouse as much as you love yourself. That is clearly something that cannot be taken lightly, this level of love leads to sacrifice. This level of love leads to binding unity. This level of love leads to a peace that will surpass all understanding and every situation and issue. This level of love is worth the effort and the peace.

DAILY PRAYER

Before you start your day, before you leave your room in the morning, hold hands and PRAY:

Lord, Your word says that if we pray in agreement and in accordance with Your will, we can have whatever it is that we ask. Lord, we admit that sometimes it's hard to hold on to our faith, especially when the answers are taking a long time. Forgive us our doubt. You have never failed our family. Help us to stand in faith, knowing that we will see the results of our commitment to You. You are the author and the finisher of our faith, so we hold on and trust You. AMEN.

DEVOTION

Marriage can so easily run off track when couples refuse to slow down for one another. Busy schedules, outside commitments, selfish ambitions and goals so often cause couples to believe they are moving forward when they are actually standing still. You can't have a conversation if no one is listening and you can't see growth in your spouse if you're not really looking. It's true that it's so much better for the relationship if you seek first to understand what your spouse is really saying before you waste your time trying to be understood.

Challenge Day Twenty-Eight Declaration

We declare and decree that as a married couple we will never forget the importance of creating a legacy of faith, love, and devotion for our children and our children's children to follow. We declare that we will lay, buy, and store up blessings for future generations. Our lives are marked by integrity and loyalty. Because we make right choices and only take steps of faith, people will seek to follow our example. Our family is surrounded by the abundance that can *only* come from a loving God.

Husband READ to Wife: Proverbs 29:20

Do you see a man hasty in his words? There is more hope for a fool than for him.

Wife READ to Husband: Ephesians 4:29

Let no corrupt word proceed out of your mouth, but what is good for necessary edification, that it may impart grace to the hearers.

MARRIAGE CHALLENGE

Go to bed early tonight. Don't go to sleep. Talk until you drift off.

Pastor Chefs Five-spice Glazed Salmon

Remember to follow this recipe to the letter. It's not about the meal; it's about the *priority time* that you spend together.

Ingredients:
¼ cup molasses
4 tsp soy sauce
1 long discussion about movies
1½ tsp five-spice powder
2 large cloves garlic, minced
1 short discussion about cartoons
1½ lbs salmon fillets
1 tbsp orange zest
1 full measure of faith (you can add this to every recipe)
Parsley or cilantro for serving

Directions:

In a small bowl, whisk the molasses, soy sauce, five-spice powder, garlic, and faith.

Put the salmon skin side down on a large plate, Pray and then pour the molasses mixture over it.

Flip the fillets so they are skin side up. Kiss your spouse. Let the fish marinate for 15 minutes at room temperature.

Position a rack 6 inches from the broiler and heat the broiler on high. Start conversation about movies. Line a large rimmed baking sheet with parchment paper (or foil coated with cooking spray).

Arrange the salmon skin side down on the baking sheet. Brush the salmon with any remaining marinade from the plate. Kiss.

Broil the salmon for 5-8 minutes until cooked (time will depend on the thickness of your fillet and how well you like your salmon cooked). Garnish with orange zest, parsley, and prayer. Love and serve hot.

What was your favorite cartoon as a child?
What's you're favorite now that you're an adult?
(it's ok to admit to your spouse that you still watch cartoons)

Day Twenty-Eight Challenge Reflection

The Pastor Chef Challenge is 40 days of praying together, reading together, and cooking together. Close the day with a *Family Declaration!* Reflect on your prayers and praise God for the day.

Praise Report:

_____

_____

_____

_____

How does today's scripture apply to your family?

_____

_____

_____

_____

How was the meal? Did you make any changes (write it down)

_____

_____

_____

_____

What is God saying to you?

_____

CHALLENGE DAY TWENTY-NINE

Submitting to one another in the fear of God.
Ephesians 5:21

In a successful marriage, both the husband and the wife realize that they are equal partners, equally responsible for the success of the relationship. The husband and the wife have to mutually agree to serve one another in love and peace. Successful marriages never lose sight of the fact that neither are the bosses and both are the servants. God commanded for the wife *and* the husband to live in submission to one another. Loving your spouse in submission opens doors of peace and lines of communication that don't exist in an environment where everyone is fighting for emotional authority.

DAILY PRAYER

Before you start your day, before you leave your room in the morning, hold hands and PRAY:

Lord, we are committed to walking with You. Show us Your ways and lead us as a couple down the trails You want us to walk. Help us, Lord, to hear Your voice guiding use where You want us to go together. We surrender our lives to You completely. We want to become more and more dependent upon Your word every single day. Help us to do what You want us to do. We trust and accept that Your ways are best, and I know that You always have our best interest in mind. AMEN.

DEVOTION

There are clear benefits to preparation and prayer. What may start off in confusion and doubt soon becomes steady, satisfied confidence in God as your renewed mind begins to rest on the promises of God. If you want to see success in your relationship with your spouse, make up your mind that you will care enough about it to wake up every morning committed to working on your relationship with God as much as you do your spouse. Every morning, as soon as you open your eyes, make up your mind to seek God's voice and humble yourself to His guidance; surrender yourself to the preparation that can only come from the Word of God.

Challenge Day Twenty-Nine Declaration

We declare and decree that God has already set the stage for our success. God has already set and assigned the right people, the right opportunities and the right solutions that will lead our family to a new level of success. No weapon formed against our family will prevail. No person, no issue, no drama can stop God's plan for us. What God has for us, is for us and nobody, anywhere, at anytime can stop it!

Husband READ to Wife: Psalms 5:3

My voice You shall hear in the morning, O Lord; In the morning I will direct it to You, And I will look up.

Wife READ to Husband: Psalms 59:16

But I will sing of Your power; Yes, I will sing aloud of Your mercy in the morning; For You have been my defense And refuge in the day of my trouble.

MARRIAGE CHALLENGE

Before you get out of the bed, pray and then sing together (no, it doesn't matter what song you sing, but sing it before you sit up).

Pastor Chefs Jerk Chicken

CHALLENGE DAY 29
PASTOR CHEFS
RECIPE
(COOK TOGETHER)

Remember to follow this recipe to the letter. It's not about the meal; it's about the *priority time* that you spend together.

Ingredients:
3-4 lbs chicken pieces
1-3 finely chopped scotch bonnet pepper (any hot pepper)
¼ cup extra virgin olive oil
3 tbsp lime juice
2 tbsp cider vinegar
2 tbsp Love
3 tbsp spiced rum
2 tbsp kosher salt
2 tbsp honesty
2 tbsp onion powder
2 tbsp dried thyme
2 tbsp allspice
2 tbsp humility
2 tbsp ground ginger
2 tbsp brown sugar
2 tbsp of kisses and hug
2 tbsp cumin
2 tbsp black pepper
2 tbsp garlic powder
2 tsp cayenne pepper

Directions:
Combine all ingredients. Don't forget to add the kisses and the hugs. This will form a paste. Coat chicken pieces with paste/marinate. Marinate for at least 4 hours, best to marinate overnight. Marinate your spouse with your love (let it sit overnight). Grill or bake chicken until chicken juices run clear.

Put any remaining jerk seasoning in zip lock bag and freeze until you need it.

Over dinner take a long walk down memory lane. Retell the story of your engagement and wedding day to each other or your children. What was the craziest, funniest, most endearing part of these milestones for you?

Day Twenty-Nine Challenge Reflection

The Pastor Chef Challenge is 40 days of praying together, reading together, and cooking together. Close the day with a *Family Declaration!* Reflect on your prayers and praise God for the day.

Praise Report:

_____

_____

_____

_____

How does today's scripture apply to your family?

_____

_____

_____

_____

How was the meal? Did you make any changes (write it down)

_____

_____

_____

_____

What is God saying to you?

_____

_____

Challenge Day Thirty

The voice of the Lord is powerful; The voice of the Lord is full of majesty.
Psalms 29:4

Have you ever heard the voice of the Lord? Do you recognize when God is talking to you specifically and directly? Does it roll in like thunder or whisper gently into your ear? God's Word and voice are awesome and powerful. God will bless you and cover you with blessings and abundance when you learn to submit to His voice and follow His will. To receive His blessings you have to first learn to hear His voice. Hearing the voice of God will help you to better respond and connect with your spouse. He will help you respond to your spouse in such a way that they will become more secure and at peace with your relationship. Hearing from God will have a powerful impact on your relationship.

DAILY PRAYER

Before you start your day, before you leave your room in the morning, hold hands and PRAY:

Lord, Our desire as a couple is to please You and hold nothing back. We surrender our relationship wholly and completely to Your will and purpose. We surrender our finances, our careers, our recreational activities, our decisions, our time, our thoughts, our bodies, and our dreams. We put them all in Your hands and for them to be used for your glory. We declare this day that we have been crucified with Christ; it is no longer us who lives, but Christ that lives in this marriage; and the life we live we commit to living in faith. Lead us, Lord, and take the lead in every area of our lives. AMEN.

DEVOTION

It never helps to play the blame game in a marriage. It leads to anger and frustration and will soon lead to unresolved anger and distance. Do you feel distant from your spouse? Search your heart for the source of that anger because everything you do will flow from the heart. Pray for peace in your spirit and for your relationship. If you have allowed distance to grow in your relationship it's time to search your motives. Let God be the bridge that brings your relationship back to the place God intended for your relationship to be from the moment He brought you together.

Challenge Day Thirty Declaration

We declare and decree that anything that doesn't line up with Your word or Your vision for our marriage is subject to deletion and change. Sickness, trouble, lack, fear, confusion, and financial difficulty are not permanent. They are temporary. We *refuse* to walk by sight, we are committed to walk by faith knowing that God will not let us down. Our marriage, our relationship, our finances, our family are all blessed. God created us and brought us together for greatness. We are ready to walk in that knowledge.

Husband READ to Wife: Psalms 37:8

Cease from anger, and forsake wrath; Do not fret—it only causes harm.

Wife READ to Husband: Ephesians 4:26

One God and Father of all, who is above all, and through all, and in you all.

Pastor Chefs Swedish Meatballs

Meatballs:
1 large yellow or white onion, peeled, grated (through a cheese grater)
2 tbsp butter
2/3 cup milk
2/3 cup of tenderness
4-5 slices of bread, crusts removed, bread cut into pieces
2 eggs
1 lb ground pork
1 1/2 lbs ground beef
2 tsp salt
2 tsp of love and spice
1 tsp freshly ground nutmeg
1 tsp ground cardamom
2 tsp black pepper

Sauce:
6 tbsp butter
1/3 cup flour
1 quart beef stock
Prayer lots and lots of prayer
1/2 to 3/4 cup sour cream
Salt
2 to 4 tbsp of raspberry jelly, more or less to taste (optional)

Directions:
Sauté the grated onion in the butter over medium-high heat until the onions soften and turn translucent, about 3-4 minutes. Pray for your spouse. Remove from heat and let cool. Give your spouse a big long emotional kiss. In a medium bowl, mix the bread pieces with the milk. Set aside for 15-20 minutes, or until the bread soaks up all the milk. When it does, pulverize the bread in a food processor and pour it into a large bowl.

Add the cooled onions to the bowl of milk and bread. Tell a joke to make your spouse laugh. Add the rest of the meatball ingredients—eggs, ground pork, ground beef, salt, nutmeg, cardamom, pepper. Using your (clean) hands, mix well for about 2 minutes until the ingredients are well combined.

Use a tbsp to measure out the meat for the meatballs. As you form the meatballs, set each one aside on a sheet pan or plate. Hug. You should get 40 to 50 meatballs. Garnish with parsley. Serve warm with a lot of love.

Remember to follow this recipe to the letter. It's not about the meal; it's about the *priority time* that you spend together.

Day Thirty Challenge Reflection

The Pastor Chef Challenge is 40 days of praying together, reading together, and cooking together. Close the day with a *Family Declaration!*
Reflect on your prayers and praise God for the day.

Praise Report:

_____

_____

_____

_____

How does today's scripture apply to your family?

_____

_____

_____

_____

How was the meal? Did you make any changes (write it down)

_____

_____

_____

_____

What is God saying to you?

_____

_____

CHALLENGE DAY THIRTY-ONE

*Not that I speak in regard to need, for I have learned in
whatever state I am, to be content.*
Philippians 4:11

Too many families spend all of their emotional energy on financial and worldly gain. They somehow believe that God's blessings always come in the form of a check or some other worldly transaction. If you are using financial gain as a barometer of your spiritual health then you are on the path to emotional and spiritual frustration and drama. If you choose to limit God's blessings for your family to a hope for wealth then you have chosen to block God's peace, love, joy, longsuffering, and grace from having an opportunity to rule in your family and relationship. Change your focus and trust God to provide the blessing in our life as He sees fit. Trust Him, He knows what He's doing.

DAILY PRAYER

Before you start your day, before you leave your room in the morning, hold hands and PRAY:
Lord, We lay our worries before You and ask for Your mighty hand to intervene and show us the path to our success and peace. Lord, we are determined to see only the good in the world around us, so we will need Your divine help not to be blinded by our own fears, doubts, wants, and preconceived ideas. Oh Lord, open our eyes that we may see Your truth in every situation. Bless us, Lord, with the ability to understand the bigger spiritual picture and to distinguish what God wants us to see from what the enemy wants to confuse us with. We trust You to bring us out of the dark and into Your divine light. AMEN.

DEVOTION

Marriages don't grow stronger during the good time; they grow stronger every time they overcome some adversity. It's during those hard times where you see God's hand on your relationship. Without the storm you will never see God silence the confusion with His word. Without the storm, you will never get to see God walk across the deep water to get to you and your family. Without the storm, you will miss the miracle. Trusting God through the storm will lead your family to a place of greater faith. Trust Him, He won't let you down.

We declare and decree that nothing is impossible for a family like ours that loves the Lord and who lives in accordance to God's will. We REFUSE to back away from our destiny because we know and believe that God has laid a solid foundation for our future. We REFUSE to sit on the side lines while God is opening doors for us to be in the game. We see each day as an opportunity to display to the world the goodness of our God and have made up our mind that we will be an example of what God can do with willing vessels!

Husband READ to Wife: 1 Corinthians 13:6

does not rejoice in iniquity, but rejoices in the truth;

Wife READ to Husband: 1 Corinthians 13:7

bears all things, believes all things, hopes all things, endures all things.

MARRIAGE CHALLENGE

Count your blessings (really count them, agree on the number).

Pastor Chefs Bacon Wrapped Salmon with Fruit Chutney

Ingredients:
8 slices center cut bacon
4 slices of affection
4 4 oz skinless salmon fillets, 1/2-inch thick
Salt and ground black pepper
1 tsp of abundance (you'll have to get this from God)
1 tsp olive oil
1/3 cup apricot jam
1 kiss (give you spouse some sugar)
1/2 cup fresh or frozen cranberries, coarsely chopped
1 tsp fresh thyme leaves

Directions:
On a microwave-safe plate lined with paper towels, microwave four slices of bacon at a time on high for 1 1/2 minutes. Kiss. Meanwhile, rinse salmon, pat dry; lightly sprinkle with salt and pepper. Pray. Wrap two bacon strips around each fillet.

In a 12-inch skillet, heat oil over medium-high heat. Love on your spouse. Cook the salmon, bacon seam-side down first, for 3 to 4 minutes per side (longer for thicker fillets) or until bacon is crisp and salmon flakes easily when tested with a fork. Make up your mind that you will enjoy the priority time you spend with your spouse.

For chutney, in a small saucepan combine jam and cranberries. Pray. Cook, stirring occasionally, over medium heat until heated through. Kiss your spouse and serve salmon with chutney and thyme.

**Over dinner take a long walk down memory lane
and keep counting your blessings…**

CHALLENGE DAY 31 PASTOR CHEFS RECIPE
(COOK TOGETHER)

Remember to follow this recipe to the letter. It's not about the meal; it's about the *priority time* that you spend together.

Day Thirty-One Challenge Reflection

The Pastor Chef Challenge is 40 days of praying together, reading together, and cooking together. Close the day with a *Family Declaration!* Reflect on your prayers and praise God for the day.

Praise Report:

_____

_____

_____

_____

How does today's scripture apply to your family?

_____

_____

_____

_____

How was the meal? Did you make any changes (write it down)

_____

_____

_____

_____

What is God saying to you?

_____

_____

CHALLENGE DAY THIRTY-TWO

...: "Fear not, for I have redeemed you; I have called you by your name;
You are Mine.
Isaiah 43:1

There is something comforting about being called by your name. It's an affirming and encouraging reminder that you are not there by accident and that you are known and recognized. How often do you and your spouse call each other by name in a way that reflects your love for them? How often do you call your spouse by name in a way to remind them that they belong and are important to you? Every time you call your spouse by name, remember that you are talking to someone that God calls special and knows them personally by name. Never forget that you belong in the kingdom and the King of ALL kings knows you personally by name.

DAILY PRAYER

Before you start your day, before you leave your room in the morning, hold hands and PRAY:
Lord, You are the author and finisher of our love for one another. You are the joy in our hearts and the peace in our spirit. Lord, teach us to love one another more deeply and to pray for one another with more passion. Thank You, Lord, for the love and emotional closeness that exist between me and my spouse. Protect our love and keep our marriage and relationship solid as we put our hope, trust and joy in You! AMEN.

DEVOTION

You can't really know God nor His goodness until you put His words into action. No matter how much you study, it is meaningless if you don't put what you read into practice. God reveals Himself and proves Himself faithful to you when you trust Him enough to make your life choices based on His word and not on your experiences. Marriage does not get stronger when you attend bible studies, marriage gets stronger when you LIVE Bible Studies.

Husband READ to Wife: Hebrew 11:1

Now faith is the substance of things hoped for, the evidence of things not seen.

Challenge Day Thirty-Two Declaration

We declare and decree that Jesus Christ is the Lord over our family and we give our lives to His leadership and guidance. We choose to live right, walk right, talk right, think right, and give right. We touch and agree that we will devote every second of our lives to pleasing our God. We know that our blessings only come from our commitment and devotion to living our lives inside of God's perfect will. We are blessed because we never give up on His will, purpose, love, and direction; we go where He leads us, and that's the end of that.

{ 138 }

Wife READ to Husband: Hebrew 11:6

But without faith it is impossible to please Him, for he who comes to God must believe that He is, and that He is a rewarder of those who diligently seek Him.

MARRIAGE CHALLENGE

In the middle of your living room, on your knees, pray for 30 minutes. (Yes, 30 full minutes on your knees praying together)

Pastor Chefs Spicy Kale and Mustard Greens

Remember to follow this recipe to the letter. It's not about the meal; it's about the *priority time* that you spend together.

Ingredients:
1 bunch mustard greens
1 prayer for your children
1 bunch kale
1 to 2 tbsp olive oil
1 prayer for your relationship
1 medium onion, chopped
12 to 16 oz andouille or Cajun-style sausage, sliced
1 tsp Cajun seasoning blend
1 prayer for your career
1/4 tsp ground black pepper
1/2 cup broth (chicken or vegetable) or water
2 cloves garlic, minced
1 prayer for your marriage
1 tbsp lemon juice
12 to 18 cherry tomatoes, sliced or halved, depending on size, or 2 medium tomatoes, diced

Directions:
Wash greens well in 2 to 3 changes of water and cut out the thick stems. Pray. Cut in 1-inch wide strips.

In a large saucepan or Dutch oven, pray and heat olive oil over medium heat. Pray. Add the onion and sausage and cook, stirring, until lightly browned. Pray. Add the Cajun seasoning and pepper, along with chicken broth or water. Pray. Add the greens and garlic and bring to a simmer. Pray. Cover and simmer for 25 minutes, stirring occasionally, until greens are very tender. Pray. Stir in the lemon juice and tomatoes and continue cooking for about 5 minutes.

Pray together... do it again.

Day Thirty-Two Challenge Reflection

The Pastor Chef Challenge is 40 days of praying together, reading together, and cooking together. Close the day with a *Family Declaration!*
Reflect on your prayers and praise God for the day.

Praise Report:

_____

_____

_____

_____

How does today's scripture apply to your family?

_____

_____

_____

_____

How was the meal? Did you make any changes (write it down)

_____

_____

_____

_____

What is God saying to you?

_____

_____

CHALLENGE DAY THIRTY-THREE

Confess your trespasses to one another, and pray for one another, that you may be healed. The effective, fervent prayer of a righteous man avails much.
James 5:16

Pray for your spouse every day. Pray openly and honestly without having any hidden secrets from your spouse. Confess your issues, fears, doubts, concerns or any other thing that your spouse may need to pray over. Part of the power in marriage is that you have someone in your life that should know all of the details about every issue you keep hidden from your friends. Confess your issues to your spouse, and then pray for one another, that you will be healed and delivered. The effective, fervent prayer of a righteous couple can overcome anything!

DAILY PRAYER

Before you start your day, before you leave your room in the morning, hold hands and PRAY:
Lord, because we are building our household on Your teachings and obeying what we have been taught, we are like the wise man that built his house on the rock. We are not like the foolish man who built his house on the sand. Lord, we are ready for the rain to come and the floods to rise because we have built our household and our relationship on Your Word. Victory is ours because our foundation is built on You. AMEN.

DEVOTION

God brings couples together in marriage so they can encourage, cheer, and console one another allowing them to accomplish things as an anointed pair that they could never accomplish alone. Ecclesiastes 4:9-10 says it best *"Two are better than one, Because they have a good reward for their labor. For if they fall, one will lift up his companion. But woe to him who is alone when he falls, For he has no one to help him up"*. That sort of says it all; couples that work together were designed by God to do GREAT things.

Challenge Day Thirty-Three Declaration

We declare and decree that we are winners and not losers. We are champions that cannot be defeated. We are over comers and much more than conquerors. We are the head and not the tail. The enemy cannot come between us because we *know* that our God has our back. We love each other with a passion that comes from knowing that God has brought us together. God has made us who we are and what we are and we are grateful.

Husband READ to Wife: Isaiah 42:9-13

Behold, the former things have come to pass, And new things I declare; Before they spring forth I tell you of them." Sing to the Lord a new song, And His praise from the ends of the earth, You who go down to the sea, and all that is in it, You coastlands and you inhabitants of them! Let the wilderness and its cities lift up their voice, The villages that Kedar inhabits. Let the inhabitants of Sela sing, Let them shout from the top of the mountains. Let them give glory to the Lord, And declare His praise in the coastlands. The Lord shall go forth like a mighty man; He shall stir up His zeal like a man of war. He shall cry out, yes, shout aloud; He shall prevail against His enemies.

Wife READ to Husband: Isaiah 43:18-19

*"Do not remember the former things, Nor consider the things of old. **Behold, I will do a new thing**, Now it shall spring forth; Shall you not know it? I will even make a road in the wilderness And rivers in the desert.*

Pastor Chefs Brown Butter Tilapia

Remember to follow this recipe to the letter. It's not about the meal; it's about the *priority time* that you spend together.

Ingredients:
1/2 cup all-purpose flour
Salt and freshly ground black pepper
2 tbsp of hope (sometimes even against all hope)
4 (3-oz) tilapia fillets
3 tbsp unsalted butter
1 cup of hot buttered praise
1 tbsp canola or peanut oil
1 big hug
1 tbsp freshly squeezed lemon juice
4 thin slices lemon, for garnish
3 tbsp roasted, salted shelled pistachios, roughly chopped

Directions:
Place flour in a shallow dish or resealable plastic bag and season with salt and pepper. Look your spouse in the eyes and declare your undying love. (make it sincere) Dredge fillets in flour mixture or add to bag, close, and shake to coat. Shake it on the dance floor. (have fun with this)

Place 1 tbsp of the butter and oil in a large frying pan over medium heat. When it foams, lower heat to medium-low. Pray.. Shake excess flour off 2 of the fillets, add to pan, add a little love and tenderness, and cook until golden brown and crisp, about 2 minutes per side. Pray. Remove fillets to a plate and repeat with remaining fillets. Kiss your spouse. Repeat the last step.

Add remaining 1 tbsp butter and cook until it begins to brown. Immediately remove from heat, stir in lemon juice, and pour over fish. Lay a lemon slice over each fillet, sprinkle pistachios over top and serve with love, prayer, mashed or roasted potatoes and a simple green salad.

**Before you sit down to eat…set the table as though it was a formal banquet, get dressed like it was a night out on the town, light some candles…
enjoy your meal.**

Day Thirty-Three Challenge Reflection

The Pastor Chef Challenge is 40 days of praying together, reading together, and cooking together. Close the day with a *Family Declaration!* Reflect on your prayers and praise God for the day.

Praise Report:

_____

_____

_____

_____

How does today's scripture apply to your family?

_____

_____

_____

_____

How was the meal? Did you make any changes (write it down)

_____

_____

_____

_____

What is God saying to you?

_____

_____

CHALLENGE DAY THIRTY-FOUR

Let all bitterness, wrath, anger, clamor, and evil speaking be put away from you, with all malice. And be kind to one another, tenderhearted, forgiving one another, just as God in Christ forgave you.
Ephesians 4:31-32

Forgiveness is the secret weapon that defeats marital confusion. Forgiveness provides freedom from the emotional bonds that keep many married couples from moving forward in the peace and freedom that they were designed to function within. Once you've chosen to accept God's gift of forgiveness, the enemy will no longer be able to use your memories as a weapon against your peace. The Lord is commanding us to put away the bitterness, wrath, anger clamor and evil conversations that rob us of our joy in a marriage. Put it away; let it go, move on… your marriage is worth it.

DAILY PRAYER

Before you start your day, before you leave your room in the morning, hold hands and PRAY:
Lord Jesus, You said that Your grace is sufficient for our marriage in any situation. When we are weak, Your power is made perfect in our relationship. We have made the decision to walk in continual humility of heart in our actions and attitude before You. We have decided to obey Your Words. We have chosen to allow our marriage to bring honor and glory to Your name, so that in our weaknesses and flaws, Your power can and will live in us. AMEN.

DEVOTION

Your willingness to forgive your spouse is the key to a happy and peaceful home. Holding on to past hurts, anger and frustration takes a lot of emotional energy that would be so much better used to build up and strengthen your marriage. Your ability to connect and grow largely depends on your ability to forgive one another as God has commanded. Loving your spouse involves, and includes, forgiving your spouse. At some point you're going to have to make up your mind that if you want a happy and positive relationship you're going to have to let some things go.

Challenge Day Thirty-Four Declaration

We declare and decree we will change the world. God brought us together as a couple to do great things in His name. God will move us ahead of others and will accelerate our dreams at a pace that will confuse the enemy. Because God love us so much He has declared in His word that "neither death nor life, nor angels nor principalities nor powers, nor things present nor things to come, nor height nor depth, nor any other created thing, shall be able to separate us from the love of God which is in Christ Jesus our Lord"… And yes, we are fully persuaded!

Husband READ to Wife: Ephesians 4:32

And be kind to one another, tenderhearted, forgiving one another, just as God in Christ forgave you.

Wife READ to Husband: Hosea 6:1

Come, and let us return to the Lord; For He has torn, but He will heal us; He has stricken, but He will bind us up.

MARRIAGE CHALLENGE

Ask your spouse for forgiveness... Forgive your spouse and forgive yourself.

Pastor Chefs Fried Catfish (you gotta love this one)

Ingredients:
2 quarts vegetable oil
1 oz of anointing oil (anoint your spouse with love)
4 whole eggs
2 cups milk
4 fillets catfish, 6 to 8 ounces each
4 moments of laughter
1 tbsp salt
1 tsp ground pepper
1 real prayer
2 cups all-purpose flour, seasoned with 1 tsp seafood seasoning
2 cups white cornmeal
1 lemon, juiced

Directions:

Heat the oil in a small fryer to 350 degrees.

Next, in a bowl, whisk together the eggs and milk, ensuring to mix well. Pray.

Then place in a shallow pan.

To bread the fish, evenly sprinkle both sides of the fillets with the salt and pepper, then dip in the seasoned flour and tap off any excess. Kiss your spouse. Follow with egg wash and finish with the cornmeal. The breading should be evenly over the fillets. Pray. Proceed to place in the heated oil and cook for 3 minutes. Hug. Then flip and finish for 2 minutes. The crust should be golden brown and crisp. Then remove from the oil and place on a paper-towel-lined platter.

To finish, kiss your spouse fully and emotionally than drizzle with lemon juice and serve.

CHALLENGE DAY 34
PASTOR CHEFS
RECIPE
(COOK TOGETHER)

Remember to follow this recipe to the letter. It's not about the meal; it's about the *priority time* that you spend together.

Day Thirty-Four Challenge Reflection

The Pastor Chef Challenge is 40 days of praying together, reading together, and cooking together. Close the day with a *Family Declaration!* Reflect on your prayers and praise God for the day.

Praise Report:

_____

_____

_____

_____

How does today's scripture apply to your family?

_____

_____

_____

_____

How was the meal? Did you make any changes (write it down)

_____

_____

_____

_____

What is God saying to you?

{ 149 }

_____

_____

CHALLENGE DAY THIRTY-FIVE

Fear not, for I am with you; I will bring your descendants from the east, And gather you from the west;
Isaiah 43:5

Fear can subtly creep into a marriage and become a quiet partner in marital decisions and choices. God did not place this spirit of fear in your marriage. God placed love for your spouse, and power to defeat the enemies to your relationship. He gave a husband and wife unity and sound minds to overcome obstacles and to chase down victory. The way to drive fear out of your household is to take your issues to God, pray together about every issue, confront them together, and move forward knowing that God is stronger than your fears. When the enemy tries to defeat you with your fears, never forget that you are not alone. You and your spouse together, with a loving, living and powerful God create an unbeatable team!

DAILY PRAYER

Before you start your day, before you leave your room in the morning, hold hands and PRAY:
Lord, thank You for replacing weariness and discouragement with Your strength, power, and renewed hope in You. As we praise You, Lord, and fellowship in Your presence, we are strengthened. Your strength causes us to soar like eagles through our life and shared responsibilities. We run hand in hand and do not grow weary. We walk together as husband and wife and do not faint. Your anointing oil flows over our heads and covers and protects us. Thank You, Lord for driving out all of our fears; we praise You and we Trust You. AMEN.

DEVOTION

A praying couple is a powerful couple. When a couple prays together in agreement there is nothing they can't accomplish because they have tapped into the power and anointing of a God that sees the impossible as possible. As a couple you can pray for wisdom and strength. Together you can bind and rebuke the enemy from placing strongholds within your family. When you notice disunity or marital struggles growing within your marriage submit to the Lord and pray together and watch the enemy flee.

Challenge Day Thirty-Five Declaration

We declare and decree spiritual abundance and breakthroughs over our family. God is moving us into a season of breakthrough where the flood of spiritual abundance will overflow our cups. We are open to God's leading and direction because we know that where God leads blessings follow. New doors and opportunities are now open to us that were once closed. New levels of favor and abundance belong to our family because we trust in His word, His direction and His plan for our household!

{ 150 }

Husband READ to Wife: Colossians 4:1

Masters, give your bondservants what is just and fair, knowing that you also have a Master in heaven.

Wife READ to Husband: Colossians 1:11-12

strengthened with all might, according to His glorious power, for all patience and longsuffering with joy; giving thanks to the Father who has qualified us to be partakers of the inheritance of the saints in the light.

MARRIAGE CHALLENGE
Share your fears with your spouse… Pray about them together.

Pastor Chefs Buffalo Chicken Wraps

Ingredients:
For the Fried Chicken Tenders:
canola oil for frying
1 cup all-purpose flour
1/4 tsp black pepper
1 tsp salt
1/2 cup buttermilk
8 chicken tenders

For the Wraps:
1/4 cup Franks Red Hot sauce
1/4 cup butter
four 12 inch wraps (I use jalapeno cheddar, though that's up to you)
1/2 head romaine lettuce, roughly chopped
1 full measure of faith
1 cup blue cheese, crumbled
1 tomato, stemmed, seeded, and chopped

Remember to follow this recipe to the letter. It's not about the meal; it's about the *priority time* that you spend together.

Directions:
For the fried chicken tenders: In a Dutch oven, pour in enough oil to come halfway up the side. Attach a deep-fry thermometer, and turn the heat to medium-high. Pray. Bring the temperature up to 350°F. Meanwhile, combine the flour, black pepper, and salt in a shallow bowl. Compliment your spouse while you pour the buttermilk into a second bowl. Add the chicken tenders to the buttermilk. Using a pair of tongs, pull up one tender and hold over the bowl to let the excess buttermilk fall back in. Sing to your spouse while you transfer the tender to the flour mixture and toss until coated. Pray. Repeat process until all the tenders are coated.

When the oil is at the right temperature, add the tenders (if they all fit in one layer) and cook until golden brown, about five minutes. Drain the tenders on paper towels when done. Pray. Repeat process if more tenders need to be cooked. Then turn off the heat.

For the wraps: In a small saucepan, melt the butter over low heat. Add the Franks hot sauce and stir until smooth. Transfer the sauce to a large bowl and add the fried chicken tenders. Hug and then toss until they are coated. Heat a large cast-iron skillet over medium heat. Add one of the wraps and let warm up for a few seconds on each side. Repeat process until all the wraps are warm.

To construct, take one wrap and add two of the sauced fried chicken tenders, a handful of romaine, a 1/4 cup of the blue cheese, and 1/4 of the chopped tomato. Fold the wrap up like a burrito, and then cut in half crosswise to serve. Pray, hug and repeat process with remaining wraps.

Day Thirty-Five Challenge Reflection

The Pastor Chef Challenge is 40 days of praying together, reading together, and cooking together. Close the day with a *Family Declaration!*
Reflect on your prayers and praise God for the day.

Praise Report:

_____

_____

_____

_____

How does today's scripture apply to your family?

_____

_____

_____

_____

How was the meal? Did you make any changes (write it down)

_____

_____

_____

_____

What is God saying to you?

_____

_____

CHALLENGE DAY THIRTY-SIX

So the Lord said to Moses, "I will also do this thing that you have spoken; for you have found grace in My sight, and I know you by name."
Exodus 33:17

God knows everything about you. He knows the good and the bad. He knows the things you are proud of as well as the things you are ashamed of admitting. God knows every detail of every story in your life. He knows your spouse just as well. "Before I formed you in the womb I knew you; Before you were born I sanctified you; I ordained you a prophet to the nations." (Jeremiah 5:1) What a satisfying thought, that He created us and called us and actually knows us by name. And because we have found grace in His sight and knows us by our names, He also responds to our prayers.

DAILY PRAYER

Before you start your day, before you leave your room in the morning, hold hands and PRAY:
Lord, help us to keep our thoughts focused on You, for You said in Your word that if our thoughts are fixed on You, You will keep us in perfect peace. You also said that righteousness would produce peace and bring joy and confidence in our marriage. Thank You, Lord, for giving us Your righteousness when we accepted Your leadership in our marriage. We trust You with our direction and our peace and the success of our relationship. AMEN.

DEVOTION

Maintaining and building a successful marriage takes work, time, and prayer. If you're not committed to putting in the work, giving your spouse the time, and spending time on your knees in prayer together, you are in for a rough ride. When times get hard, it is so easy to start pointing fingers and laying blame for your marital issues. Resist the urge to do anything at all with your problems and concerns before you take them to God in prayer. Never underestimate the power or prayer; never underestimate God's ability to make the impossible, possible. There is *nothing* in your marriage that is too hard for God to fix, if you trust Him.

Challenge Day Thirty-Six Declaration

We declare and decree that God called our family directly and specifically to do great things in His name. He brought us together for legacy and purpose. God is opening doors that have been closed and moving obstacles that have blocked our way in the past. God is giving us favor with people who will be able to help us achieve our goal. God's abundance surrounds our family and will be the legacy that we leave future generations.

Husband READ to Wife: Mark 11:24

Therefore I say to you, whatever things you ask when you pray, believe that you receive them, and you will have them.

Wife READ to Husband: James 5:15

And the prayer of faith will save the sick, and the Lord will raise him up. And if he has committed sins, he will be forgiven.

MARRIAGE CHALLENGE

Before you go to bed, get on your knees together and pray… do it again.

Pastor Chefs Bruschetta Chicken

Remember to follow this recipe to the letter. It's not about the meal; it's about the *priority time* that you spend together.

Ingredients:
3 or 4 chicken breasts
4 or 5 small tomatoes, chopped
2 BIG hugs (real hugs not pity pat hugs)
1 clove garlic, minced
1/2 small red onion, chopped
1 full embrace that accurately expresses your Love
1 tsp olive oil
1 tsp balsamic vinegar
1/8 tsp sea salt
Handful basil, chopped

Directions:
Preheat oven to 375 degrees F (if you choose to bake your chicken rather than grill). Pray and then sprinkle some salt and pepper over top, cover and bake for about 35 to 40 minutes (depending on the size of your breasts) until juices run clear.

Meanwhile, combine chopped tomatoes, garlic, onion, olive oil, balsamic vinegar, sea salt and basil in a bowl. Hug. Hug again. Refrigerate until chicken is ready to be served and spoon over top of the chicken.

Day Thirty-Six Challenge Reflection

The Pastor Chef Challenge is 40 days of praying together, reading together, and cooking together. Close the day with a *Family Declaration!* Reflect on your prayers and praise God for the day.

Praise Report:

_____

_____

_____

_____

How does today's scripture apply to your family?

_____

_____

_____

_____

How was the meal? Did you make any changes (write it down)

_____

_____

_____

_____

What is God saying to you?

_____

_____

CHALLENGE DAY THIRTY-SEVEN

...let each one of you in particular so love his own wife as himself, and let the wife see that she respects her husband.
Ephesians 5:33

A healthy Christian marriage should create an environment where both the husband and the wife feel safe and loved. A wife wants to know that her husband loves her with all his heart, complete and sacrificially. A husband wants to know that not only does his wife love him but respect his hard work and commitment to his family. A healthy Christian marriage should be one where both spouses can worship God with all their heart and all their soul knowing that they are completely safe to be themselves. God uses marriage to help us grow and become the man/woman that He created us to be. For God, even our marriage is a tool to make us better.

DAILY PRAYER

Before you start your day, before you leave your room in the morning, hold hands and PRAY:
Lord, in the name of Jesus we take authority over any spirit of confusion and doubt that may attempt to find a place in our home. Lord we release into our home an anointing that brings peace, love, joy, longsuffering, and a confident attitude that comes from knowing You have a plan and purpose for our family. Lord, thank You for bringing our family together and moving us into a place of prosperity and peace. AMEN.

DEVOTION

The bible tells us that Iron sharpens Iron, but it can also be said that husbands and wives sharpen each other and help each other grow spiritually and emotionally. Through words of encouragement, emotional support, and sincere prayer, spouses lift one another up. Being a true encouragement for your spouse takes time and commitment. When we take a real interest in seeing how God moves in the lives of our spouses and families, our faith is encouraged even the more. As we allow God to strengthen us, we become more useful and effective tools for sharpening each other and growing together.

Challenge Day Thirty-Seven Declaration

We declare and decree that no weapon formed against our family shall prosper. And declare that any and every tongue that rises up against us shall be condemned. God has given us a heritage of victory that future generations shall use as an example. God has made us a royal priesthood, a chosen generation, a peculiar family that praises the name of the Lord at all times. There are no limits to what we can do because we have God on our side.

Husband READ to Wife: Proverbs 27:17

As iron sharpens iron, So a man sharpens the countenance of his friend.

Wife READ to Husband: Ephesians 5:21

Submitting to one another in the fear of God.

MARRIAGE CHALLENGE

If tomorrow was the last day you had on earth with your spouse, what would you do? Do that.

Pastor Chefs White Chicken Chili

CHALLENGE DAY 37
PASTOR CHEFS
RECIPE
(COOK TOGETHER)

Remember to follow this recipe to the letter. It's not about the meal; it's about the *priority time* that you spend together.

Ingredients:

1 lb boneless skinless chicken breasts, diced into 1/2-inch pieces
1 small yellow onion, diced
1 small hug (not a big one..just one to get you through the meal)
1 tbsp olive oil
2 cloves garlic, finely minced
2 (14.5 oz) cans chicken broth
1 (4 oz) can diced green chilies
1 1/2 tsp cumin
3/4 tsp paprika
1/2 tsp dried oregano
1/2 tsp ground coriander
1/4 tsp cayenne pepper
1 full measure of faith (1 is all you need)
salt and freshly ground black pepper, to taste
1 (8 oz) pkg Neufchatel cheese, cut into 12 slices (aka light cream cheese)
1 1/4 cup fresh corn (frozen works too)
2 (15 oz) cans cannellini beans, drained and rinsed
1 tbsp fresh lime juice
chopped fresh cilantro, for serving
shredded Monterrey Jack cheese, for serving
tortilla chips, for serving (optional)

Directions:

Heat olive oil in a 6 quart enameled dutch oven over medium-high heat. Once oil is hot add chicken and diced onion and saute until chicken is no longer pink, about 6 minutes. Pray. Add garlic and saute 30 seconds longer. Add chicken broth, green chilies, cumin, paprika, oregano, coriander, cayenne pepper and season with salt and pepper to taste. Hug. Bring mixture just to a boil then reduce heat and simmer 15 minutes.

Add Neufchatel (or cream) cheese and stir until nearly melted (it will break down in little bits and will appear to look like separated cheese but it will eventually melt). Pray. Stir in corn, and 1 can of Cannellini beans, then process 3/4 of the remaining beans along with 1/4 cup broth from the soup in a food processor until pureed, add bean mixture to soup along with remaining 1/4 can of beans (you can skip the pureeing step and just add the beans directly to soup, the soup just won't be quite as creamy). Simmer for about 15 minutes longer hug your spouse while you wait. Mix in fresh lime juice and serve with Monterrey Jack cheese, chopped cilantro and tortilla chips for dipping if desired.

Day Thirty-Seven Challenge Reflection

The Pastor Chef Challenge is 40 days of praying together, reading together, and cooking together. Close the day with a *Family Declaration!* Reflect on your prayers and praise God for the day.

Praise Report:

_____

_____

_____

_____

How does today's scripture apply to your family?

_____

_____

_____

_____

How was the meal? Did you make any changes (write it down)

_____

_____

_____

_____

What is God saying to you?

_____

_____

CHALLENGE DAY THIRTY-EIGHT

Therefore comfort one another with these words.
1 Thessalonians 4:18

God loves when we let Him fight our battles. He loves when we trust Him enough to let Him take the lead in our homes. God loves when we drop to our knees as a husband and wife and go to battle in prayer. When we love one another enough to enter spiritual warfare as two people, we become a single powerful spiritual warrior that the enemy fears. Our connection in prayer generates power that shakes the very foundation of the enemy and brings blessings and power to our entire family. Prayer is the difference between you fighting for yourself and God fighting for your family. When you let God fight for you, YOU WIN.

DAILY PRAYER

Before you start your day, before you leave your room in the morning, hold hands and PRAY:
Lord, we thank You that You are a God of renewal and restoration. Thank You, Lord, for being our strength when we feel weak. Thank You for injecting Your spiritual perfection into our many imperfections. Help us, Lord, to remember You when times get hard. Help us, Lord, to push through relationship issues, emotional frustration, career issues, and any other trick the enemy attempts to use to break our marriage. Lord, we trust You and depend on You for our strength. AMEN.

DEVOTION

Men change. Women change. People change. God has given us a powerful and wonderful opportunity to grow and change with our spouses. It is a blessing to be able to grow and change with your spouse. Your relationship will grow and change. Your finances will grow and change. Your thoughts and opinions about life will grow and change. God called you to work and function as one person, growing and changing together. Don't ignore the changes, thank God for them and grow! Growth REQUIRES change.

Challenge Day Thirty-Eight Declaration

We declare and decree that all of the things that used to scare us now encourage us. The things that used to break us now strengthen us. The things that used to confuse us not teach us. Lord we thank You for using our weaknesses to make us stronger. Lord we praise You for bringing us into a place where our confidence is focused on You and not on our problems. We declare that no matter what we go through, You will always bring us through stronger than we started and more focused on Your Word.

Husband READ to Wife: Ephesians 5:15-17

See then that you walk circumspectly, not as fools but as wise, redeeming the time, because the days are evil. Therefore do not be unwise, but understand what the will of the Lord is.

Wife READ to Husband: 1 Peter 3:8

Finally, all of you be of one mind, having compassion for one another; love as brothers, be tenderhearted, be courteous;

MARRIAGE CHALLENGE

Rate your relationship on a scale of one to ten, If it's not a ten, discuss what you need to do to make it better. Ask God to help.

Pastor Chefs BBQ Chicken Salad

CHALLENGE DAY 38
PASTOR CHEFS
RECIPE
(COOK TOGETHER)

Remember to follow this recipe to the letter. It's not about the meal; it's about the *priority time* that you spend together.

Ingredients:
1 tbsp olive oil
2 boneless, skinless thin-sliced chicken breasts
Kosher salt and freshly ground black pepper, to taste
6 cups chopped romaine lettuce
1 peck on the cheek
1 Roma tomato, diced
3/4 cup canned corn kernels, drained
3/4 cup canned black beans, drained and rinsed
1/4 cup diced red onion
1 full prayer for the marriage
1/4 cup shredded Monterey Jack cheese
1/2 cup shredded cheddar cheese
1/4 cup Ranch dressing
2 cup love and tenderness (yes, you'll need both)
1/4 cup BBQ sauce
1/4 cup tortilla strips

Directions:

Heat olive oil in a medium skillet over medium high heat.

Season chicken breasts with salt and pepper, to taste. Kiss your spouse (to taste) Add to skillet and cook, flipping once, until cooked through, about 3-4 minutes per side. Pray. Let cool before dicing into bite-size pieces.

To assemble the salad, place romaine lettuce in a large bowl; top with tomato, corn, beans, onion and cheeses. Kiss and then pour ranch dressing and BBQ sauce on top of the salad and gently toss to combine.

Serve immediately after you passionately kiss your spouse. Top with tortilla strips (the salad not the kiss).

Day Thirty-Eight Challenge Reflection

The Pastor Chef Challenge is 40 days of praying together, reading together, and cooking together. Close the day with a *Family Declaration!* Reflect on your prayers and praise God for the day.

Praise Report:

_____

_____

_____

_____

How does today's scripture apply to your family?

_____

_____

_____

_____

How was the meal? Did you make any changes (write it down)

_____

_____

_____

What is God saying to you?

_____

_____

CHALLENGE DAY THIRTY-NINE

I am my beloved's, And his desire is toward me.
Song of Solomon 7:10

Do you remember the moment that you fell in love with your spouse? Do you remember the butterflies? Do you remember those bubbling emotions you felt after that first kiss from your beloved? Think about the qualities that first attracted you to your spouse. Was it their smile? Was it their sense of humor? Was it their confident attitude? Was it their prayer life and devotion to God? Take a moment and imagine those moments and those thoughts and fall in love with your spouse all over again. You can do it, if you try. Like everything else in life, love must grow or it will surely die.

DAILY PRAYER

Before you start your day, before you leave your room in the morning, hold hands and PRAY:

Lord, we trust You with our love and our relationship. Lord, we trust You with our passions, hopes and dreams. Lord, we refuse to lean on our own understanding and acknowledge You in all of our ways. Lord, we need You to guide and lead us. Lord, we need You to direct our path and provide direction for our family. Lord, we ask that You order our steps and take charge of our marriage. Help us, Lord, to do all that we need to do to keep our love for one another alive. AMEN.

DEVOTION

Admitting our faults to one another is an important part of the marriage relationship. Living with your spouse naked and exposed is as vital to a marriage as food and water is to the body. Pretending to be healthy doesn't make you healthy nor does pretending to be happy in a marriage make you happy. Couples must admit their weaknesses and flaws to heal and grow. Couples must be transparent to one another in ways that allow for growth and sincere emotional development. The Bible says "The truth will set you free!" Married couples who are open and allow themselves to be vulnerable to one another are free to be themselves. Wow, that's free indeed.

Challenge Day Thirty-Nine Declaration

We declare and decree that my spouse and I are world changers and people builders. We look for opportunities to lift people up and to improve their world through encouragement and prayer. We speak words of faith, love, victory, and power into the lives of the people around us, reminding them that they are special in the eyes of a mighty and loving God. We plant seeds of peace in our workplace and anoint our children with love and joy. We desire to be the change the world needs and surrender our lives for God to use.

Husband READ to Wife: Proverbs 2:3-4

Yes, if you cry out for discernment, And lift up your voice for understanding, If you seek her as silver, And search for her as for hidden treasures;

Wife READ to Husband: 1 Corinthians 13:6-7

does not rejoice in iniquity, but rejoices in the truth; bears all things, believes all things, hopes all things, endures all things.

MARRIAGE CHALLENGE

Dare to risk the awkward moments for your relationship. Play truth or dare.
(Have fun with this)

Pastor Chefs Cheesy Chicken and Potato Chowder

Ingredients:

4 cups chicken broth
2 cups (2 medium) diced peeled potatoes
2 cups of joy
1 cup (2-3 medium) diced carrots
1 cup (3 medium stalks) diced celery
1/2 cup diced onion
1 full heaping cup of honesty
1 1/2 tsp kosher salt
1/2 tsp black pepper
1 tsp dried thyme
1 cup praise
1/4 cup unsalted butter
1/3 cup all-purpose flour
2 cups milk (I used skim)
2 cups (8 oz.) shredded cheddar cheese
2 cups diced cooked chicken
1/4 cup chopped fresh parsley

Remember to follow this recipe to the letter. It's not about the meal; it's about the *priority time* that you spend together.

Directions:

In a 4-quart saucepan, bring chicken broth to a boil. Reduce heat; add the potatoes, carrots, joy, celery, onion, salt, love, pepper and thyme. Pray and then cover and simmer for 15 minutes, or until vegetables are tender.

Meanwhile, melt butter in a medium saucepan over medium-high heat. Whisk in flour until smooth. Gradually whisk in milk. Hug one another while you bring to a boil and stir for 2 minutes, or until thickened. Reduce heat and add cheese, stirring until melted. Stir cheese mixture and shredded chicken into broth. Cook and stir until heated through.

Ladle into serving bowls. Hug, kiss and sprinkle with chopped parsley.

Day Thirty-Nine Challenge Reflection

The Pastor Chef Challenge is 40 days of praying together, reading together, and cooking together. Close the day with a *Family Declaration!* Reflect on your prayers and praise God for the day.

Praise Report:

_____

_____

_____

_____

How does today's scripture apply to your family?

_____

_____

_____

_____

How was the meal? Did you make any changes (write it down)

_____

_____

_____

_____

What is God saying to you?

_____

_____

CHALLENGE DAY FORTY

My brethren, count it all joy when you fall into various trials.
James 4:1-2

Every marriage is full of challenges and frustration. Every marriage faces hardships and trials. God wants us to consider our trials and frustrations as joy. God wants us to develop an attitude which allows the negative circumstances that happen within our marriage to affect us positively. God wants us to make the choice to trust Him enough to get us through our circumstances with joy in our hearts and spirits. Make up your mind that you will trust God so much that when negative circumstances come against your marriage, you're able to praise God for the opportunity to grow together as a couple knowing that even when the situation feels out of control, God has your situation well at hand.

DAILY PRAYER

Before you start your day, before you leave your room in the morning, hold hands and PRAY:

Oh Lord, today we confess that our lives are complete in You, Lord Jesus. That means we trust You for every answer, every need, and every solution to every question that we may have. Thank You, for empowering us to do great things together as husband and wife. Thank You, for allowing us to draw strength from Your Word and from Your love. You are everything that we need and everything that we want. We thank You for Your thoughts and plans for peace in our marriage. Thank You, Lord for making our lives complete. Thank You for bringing us together. AMEN.

DEVOTION

A successful marriage takes more than one act of kindness or one act of devotion. A successful marriage takes thousands of little moments strung together to form one single happy relationship. Displaying a particular trait once or twice is not a habit, exhibiting a trait over and over again until it becomes a natural part of you is when a habit begins to form. Showing love for your spouse should become a habit. Talking to your spouse and sharing your life and adventures with your spouse should become a habit. Praying with your spouse should become a habit. Trusting God for miracles together as husband and wife should become a habit. A successful marriage requires a lot of good habits. Trust God.

Challenge Day Forty Declaration

We declare and decree that pleasing our God and the success of this marriage is our highest priority. Anything that doesn't line up with God's vision for this marriage will be cast aside and rejected. Every person that brings confusion or generates doubt in this relationship will be rebuked. We are devoted to this marriage and to one another. We are sold out to God's purpose and direction. We will become the people God created us to be and will produce and live in the marriage that God modeled for us to live in. We refuse to live or accept anything less than God's best.

Husband READ to Wife: James 1:19-20

So then, my beloved brethren, let every man be swift to hear, slow to speak, slow to wrath; for the wrath of man does not produce the righteousness of God.

Wife READ to Husband: Galatians 5:22-23

But the fruit of the Spirit is love, joy, peace, longsuffering, kindness, goodness, faithfulness, gentleness, self-control. Against such there is no law.

Pastor Chefs Garlic-Lemon Double Stuffed Chicken

Remember to follow this recipe to the letter. It's not about the meal; it's about the *priority time* that you spend together.

Ingredients:
oil, for greasing pan
8 boneless, skinless chicken breast halves
1 prayer for your marriage
1 (8 oz) package cream cheese, cut into 1/2 inch slices
1 (8 oz) package Cheddar cheese, cut into 1/2 inch slices
1 cup milk
1cup love and kindness
1 1/2 cups Italian seasoned bread crumbs
1/2 cup grated Romano cheese
1 tbsp minced garlic
1 cup emotional availability
3/4 cup butter, melted
2 tbsp lemon juice
1/2 tsp garlic salt, or to taste
1/2 tsp paprika (optional)

Directions:
Preheat oven to 350 degrees F (175 degrees C). Lightly coat a large, shallow baking dish with oil.

Butterfly each breast by slicing in half horizontally through the center, cutting almost but not completely through. Place one slice each of Cheddar and cream cheese in the center of each breast. Pray. Close again as if placing between the pages of a book. Set aside.

Hug your spouse than pour milk into a shallow bowl. In a separate bowl, combine breadcrumbs and Romano cheese. Prayerfully and carefully dip each breast first in milk, then in breadcrumb mixture, patting lightly to firmly coat. Place breasts side by side in a single layer in pre-oiled baking dish, tucking edges under to seal.

Melt butter in a small saucepan over medium heat. Kiss and then stir in lemon juice and garlic, and drizzle evenly over chicken. Season breasts with garlic salt and paprika, if using.

Bake in preheated oven for 30 min. or until no longer pink in center and juices run clear. (can you hold your spouse for 30 min. while you wait?)

Day Forty Challenge Reflection

The Pastor Chef Challenge is 40 days of praying together, reading together, and cooking together. Close the day with a *Family Declaration!* Reflect on your prayers and praise God for the day.

Praise Report:

_____

_____

_____

_____

How does today's scripture apply to your family?

_____

_____

_____

_____

How was the meal? Did you make any changes (write it down)

_____

_____

_____

_____

What is God saying to you?

_____

_____

Congratulations!

You have officially completed the 40 days of challenge.

This challenge was designed to press you and your spouse to spend quality and priority time together.

Unrealistic Expectations

There is a growing trend today where being too busy to enjoy life has become more the rule of thumb rather than the exception. Between work, school, children, hobbies, outside friendships and relationship it's a wonder that many couples still use the term married at all. I've noticed that way too many married couples have grown comfortable living as two ships that pass in the night. Whether it's work or play, the goal seems to be the same: stay busy. It's been taught by too many pastors, ministers, and educators that productivity and constant activity is the key to happiness—living under a cloud of fear that "life is too short" and "if you don't hurry, you'll miss something." The problem with this *stay busy* philosophy is that it has an unfortunate and inherent consequence of turning activity into an empty shell of a relationship where a couple spends more time PRETENDING to love one another than actually loving one another.

With all this being said, we still expect our spouses or significant others to be our best friend and soulmate. We still expect to have and maintain a *deeper* connection without putting in *deeper* connecting time. It's honestly a lot to expect for you to maintain this *deeper* level of love and romantic attachment when the kids are sick, the car is acting up, and you're scared you may lose your job at any moment. The things that were once quality-time activities are now chores on your to-do list… How do you turn the tide on this trend? How do you generate quality moments without taking a vacation? How do you find an activity that will generate quality time while also meeting the needs of your household? How do you change your attitude? The answer is **Priority Time**!

Never forget that marriage is not a fantasy; marriage is *not* a covenant love affair; it is a covenant *bond* where God forms one person out of two. God gave the married couple responsibilities and expectations to build and lead future generations together. In other words, God gave them a job. God did not expect them to just coast into peace and harmony. *Successful marriages take work… And sometimes… they take a lot of hard work.*

There is no magic to success; there is just commitment and clarity that God put you and your spouse together. After 30 years of marriage, I've come to realize that love, combined with a little stubbornness and **priority time,** can go a long way to helping you get through the hard times.

This is not the end, if you've completed the challenge and want to continue to spend time with your spouse in the kitchen, feel free to look for more pastor chef recipes on Facebook: https://www.facebook.com/PastorChefs (this is how marriages grow stronger… they pray together…they read together…and they *cook* together).

We hope you enjoyed *Pastor Chefs 40 Day Marriage Challenge* and that you found it helpful and rewarding in blessing your marriage.

For similar uplifting books from Signalman Publishing, please visit out website at www.signalmanpublishing.com.

Bulk orders are available for discount direct from the publisher. Please contact via email: info@signalmanpublishing.com.

 SIGNALMAN PUBLISHING

CPSIA information can be obtained
at www.ICGtesting.com
Printed in the USA
LVOW01s2244221115

463755LV00019B/354/P